The Radical Gospel of Paul

and

Christian Scripture

Dennis Lines

Copyright © Dennis Lines 2019

All Publishing Rights

Apart from any fair dealing for the purposes of research or private study, or criticism or review, as permitted under the Copyright, Designs and Patents Act, 1988, this publication may be reproduced, stored or transmitted in any form, or by any means, only with the prior permission in writing of the publisher, or in the case of reprographic reproduction, in accordance with the terms of licences issued by the Copyright Licensing Agency. Enquiries concerning reproduction outside those terms should be sent to the publisher.

All photographs and maps reproduced in this book are in the public domain and are therefore outside copyright conditions. Any outstanding rights and permissions, please make contact with the author at this address.

Published by:
Dennis Lines
1 Holywell Lane
Rubery
Birmingham B45 9EJ
daimlerden@icloud.com

The Radical Gospel of Paul and Christian Scripture can be purchased directly from the author/publisher.

British Library Cataloguing in publication data:

A catalogue record for this book is available from the British library: ISBN 978-0-9550831-3-6

Front Cover: *Conversión de Saulo*, Caravaggio, c. 1615–1620.

To those travellers who know the value of Christian Spirituality, who have taken the road of rational empiricism and have gained the wisdom to appreciate the importance of both.

Augustus or Jesus: Emperor or Christ?

Maecenas Presenting the Liberal Arts to Emperor Augustus, Giovanni Tiepolo, 1743
Below Left: *Salvator Mundi* (*Saviour* of the World), Leonardo da Vinci, 1452-1519
Below Right: *Death on a Pale Horse*, William Blake, *c.* 1800 (Revelation 19:13-16)

Contents

Chronological Tables

Introduction	1
1. Caesar Augustus: Saviour of the World	9
2. Constantine Becomes a Christian	19
3. A Tale of Two Saviours	33
4. Paul: A Light to the Nations	49
5. The Gentle Controversy	63
6. From Jewish Prophet to God	87
7. Contradictions in the Gospels	109
8. Forged Christian Documents	123
9. Towards a Theology of the Bible	143
Afterthought	167
Subject and Author Index	171
Biblical Page Index	173
References	175

Dates of Paul's Mission: Mainline Scholarship

−43	Augustus Emperor 43 BCE–4 CE	
−4	Birth of Jesus	
14	Tiberius Emperor 14–37	
30–33	Jesus crucified	
32–34	Paul converted	
33/34	Paul in Arabia 33–37?	
37	Gaius (Caligula) Emperor 37–41	
37	Paul in Damascus	
38	Paul to Tarsus and Antioch	
41	Claudius Emperor 41–54	
41–45?	Paul and Barnabas: Mission 1	
48–49	Apostolic Assembly	
48	Peter in Antioch	
49–50	Paul and Silas: Mission 2	
49	Claudius expels rioters from Rome	
49–51	Paul in Corinth	1 Thessalonians
53–54	Paul's imprisonment at Ephesus	1 Corinthians, Galatians
54	Nero Emperor 54–68	
55	Paul: Mission 3	
55–56	Paul in Macedonia and Achaia	
56–57	Paul in Jerusalem (Spring)	2 Corinthians
58	Paul in prison at Caesarea	
59	Paul's Journey to Rome	
60	Shipwreck at Malta	
60–	Paul in Rome under house arrest	Philemon, Philippians
63–64	Paul's martyrdom under Nero	Romans
64	Fire of Rome	2 Thessalonians?
66–73	Jewish uprising	Hebrews? Mark?
69	Vespasian Emperor 69–79	Ephesians?
70	Fall of Jerusalem	Colossians?
79	Titus Emperor 79–81	Matthew? Luke?
81	Domitian Emperor 81–96	Revelation?
98	Trajan Emperor 98–117	John? Acts?

95–10	Deutero-Pauline Documents	*1 & 2 Timothy? Titus?*
95–150	Apocryphal Christian Documents	*1 & 2 Peter?*
117	Hadrian Emperor (117–138)	*Gospel of Peter 130?*
312	Battle at the Milvian Bridge	*Apocalypse of Peter 150?*
312	Conversion of Constantine	
313	Edict of Milan cessation of Christian persecution	
324	Constantine Emperor 306–337	
324	Eusebius: *Church Histories*	
325	Council of Nicaea	
379	Theodosius I Emperor 379–395	
402	Theodosius II Emperor 402–450	

Dates of Paul's Mission: Tom Wright's Version

33	Paul in Jerusalem	
33–36	Paul in Arabia	
37	Paul in Damascus	
38	Paul to Tarsus and Antioch	
47–48	Paul in Jerusalem: Mission 1	
48	Peter in Antioch	*Galatians*
48/49	Apostolic Conference	
49	Paul and Silas: Mission 2	
51–52	Paul in Corinth, then Jerusalem	*1 & 2 Thessalonians*
52/53	Paul in Antioch: Mission 3	
53–56	Paul in Ephesus	*1 Corinthians*
53/54	Paul's painful visit to Corinth	*Philippians, Philemon &*
53/54	Imprisonment at Ephesus	*Ephesians, 2 Corinthians & Colossians*
55/57	Release from Prison at Ephesus	*Romans*
56–57	Paul in Corinth and Jerusalem	
62–64	Paul to Spain and on: Mission 4	*1 & 2 Timothy and Titus*
64	Paul's martyrdom under Nero	

Christian Persecution by Roman Emperors

30–33 CE	Under Tiberius, the Judean Prefect crucifies Jesus of Nazareth.
49	Claudius expels Jews and Jewish Christians from Rome.
64	Nero sets Christians ablaze as scapegoats for the fire in Rome.
161–180?	Marcus Aurelius torches Christians in two cities of Gaul (modern France) and enforces many to recant of their newfound faith.
195–251?	Decius punishes local Christians for refusing to offer animal sacrifices to the gods and join in Roman ceremonies.
257	Valerian persecutes local Christians in Rome for refusing to take part in pagan rituals, outlaws covert meetings in cemeteries. and executes bishops, presbyters and deacons.
303	Diocletian decrees all Christian meetings illegal: Christian places of worship are destroyed and Christian writings are confiscated. Those of high social status lose their rank, and Christian freedmen in imperial service are re-enslaved. A further decree was issued to arrest the clergy, and a later edict in the spring of 304 required everyone in the Empire to gather in public places and participate in animal sacrifices.
312	Constantine converts from paganism to Christianity.
313	Constantine and Licinius issue the Edict of Toleration.
325	Constantine rules over the Council of Bishops in Nicaea.
341	Constantius II issues legislation banning all pagan practices.
361	Julian suppresses Christianity for 19 months in an attempt to reinstate paganism in place of Christianity.
363	The Christian emperor Jovian replaces Julian, and from then on there would never be a pagan ruler of the Roman Empire.
391–392	Theodosius I decreed pagan practices illegal and in effect established Christianity as the religion of the Empire. The Theodosian Code was later issued by Theodosius II in 429.

Introduction

We are to study the conversion of a Jew called Saul, who is confronted by a deceased Galilean on the road to Damascus, an apparition of the Jewish prophet, Yeshua bar Joseph (Jesus of Nazareth): Jesus had been crucified in the 30s by the Roman governor of the province of Judea.[A] Saul is more commonly referred to by his Greek name Paul after he became an apostle of Christ.[1] We also present an account of the Radical Gospel he preached to Greco-Roman pagans during the early first century.

The Pre-Christian Saul

Paul has sometimes been stigmatised as an impulsive Mediterranean Jew who was anti-female, pro-slavery and an idealistic proponent of the Jesus movement. Our search for the historical Paul, before Christian Scripture emerged, claims that such characterisations misrepresent what Paul was like during the active period of his life.

Saul became a Jewish rabbi and a Pharisee of the diaspora. The Pharisees during the 80s, when Luke wrote Acts, became more pious and exclusive than their fathers had been during the times of Jesus in the 30s. Matthew was to ridicule the missionary endeavours of Pharisees to make converts twice as much *children of hell* as themselves, an indictment that says more about the evangelist than the historical Jesus.[B] Palestinian Pharisees were much less tolerant than those of the diaspora after the Second Temple fell to Rome in 70 CE. Judean Pharisees in the days of Saul were insistent that Gentile converts to the Jesus movement were to be circumcised. Clashes between conservative and liberal Jews took place. Clearly, Saul of Tarsus belonged to that conservative wing of Judaism which insisted that Jewish converts to Jesus were to be circumcised, to honour the Sabbath day, and to follow the kosher dietary codes prescribed in the Torah (Jewish Law).[C]

[A] John 1:45
[B] Matthew 23:15
[C] Galatians 5:11

But everything changed when Jesus was revealed to Saul shortly after the resurrection.[2]

The Social World of Paul

Little is known of Saul's early days, other than that he came from Tarsus. Tarsus was 'no mean city' of Greco-Roman culture and was well situated along the Mediterranean coast at the foot of the Taurus Mountains on the main route over high passes from Asia Minor to Syria. Although not very significant today, in Saul's time Tarsus had been a flourishing Hellenistic city that was ideally placed for trade and commerce.[A]

When Saul of Tarsus converted, it was a time of upheaval in the Empire. The Greek city-state system of government failed, the deities of antiquity were questioned, and esoteric religions from the East were synchronised within Greco-Roman religion. Hebrew Scripture had been translated into Greek at Alexandria and became the preferred text in the synagogues of

---

[A] Acts 21:39 KJV

the diaspora. Educated Jewish philosophers (such as Philo of Alexandria) began to integrate Jewish teachings with Hellenistic philosophy, but 'the stricter Jewry of Palestine entered a ghetto of its own choice' by rejecting the Jewish and Christian philosophies coming out of Alexandria.[3] Within this political culture of religion and superstition we are to locate Paul and his Radical Gospel to Greco-Roman Gentiles.

The Jewish Diaspora under the Roman Empire

The Christian mission to proselytise the Gentiles was not entirely unique. Diaspora Jews believed they had a responsibility from Deutero-Isaiah to be a 'light to the nations'.[A] Luke, in the book of Acts, writes about pagan sympathisers who were being drawn to Judaism at the local synagogues. The Hellenistic rulers granted the Jews extensive rights of incorporation, protection in law and special privileges, and Roman rulers took the same attitude. First-century Jews had rights to practise their own religious and cultic ceremonies without molestation, to manage their communities and own property. The Jews had been exempted from Emperor worship, and military service, owing to the strictures over the Sabbath. Given that the Jews represented only 7% of the population during the time of Caesar Augustus (about 4.5 million), and that they were free to practise Judaism, we must account for the high numbers of Jewish and Gentile conversions to the Jesus movement in the Mediterranean regions and northern Egypt during the first century.[4]

Why did Christianity prove so popular in the fourth century to become the principal religion of the Empire? Social historians have addressed the question, and come up with a range of geographic and political solutions, including the relative ease of travel through the Mediterranean, and the scattered synagogues throughout the Roman Empire. Political factors, no doubt, assisted the early Christian missionaries to achieve unprecedented success in spreading the message, but, whatever the reason, the relentless endeavours of small groups of converted Jews from the diaspora, such as Saul of Tarsus, have to be considered a significant factor.

[A] Isaiah 42:6, 49:1–7; Acts 26:15–18

Source Material

We attempt to locate Paul within the Mediterranean world of the Roman Empire of the first century. To do otherwise runs the risk of reading into his life and ministry notions of a modern perspective. This is no easy task for two reasons: the primary sources of the life and theology of Paul are found in the earliest Christian writings, but there are different projections of Paul in the New Testament. To construct a systematic theology of Paul from Christian works is a daunting endeavour in itself; even compiling a chronology of his life is not straightforward.

The conventional resource for study of Paul's ministry has traditionally been Acts, but it is a matter of great surprise that not a single passage in Luke's writing shows an awareness of Paul's letters, or use of them. This implies that at the time when Acts appeared there was no representative collection of Paul's letters in the Christian assemblies.[5]

Acts appeared when the conflict between Jewish and Gentile Christians over the validity of the Law, circumcision and kosher was resolved. That confrontation between converted Jewish Christians and pagans entering the Jesus community was in Luke's day a distant memory. We don't find, therefore, the same discord and passionate exchanges in Acts as is found in Paul's letters to the Galatians and Romans. I will prioritise the primary sources of personal testimony in the letters of Paul over the retrospective use of them by Luke where there is disagreement or different emphases.

Acts was written after the Gospel of Luke, and should be placed closer to the 90s than the 80s. It must not be used uncritically to supplement or to confirm the authentic sources of Paul's letters: there are contradictions in historical details between them. The service done in recent research over Pauline study is to reveal the questionable methodology of synchronising sources in Acts with those in the letters of Paul. Harmonising divergent records results in blurring the contours of the picture of Paul as he was in life, and in damaging our understanding of the historical and theological problems connected with his Gospel and mission.[6] However, to recognise the discrepancies does not in the least suggest that Acts has no historical value, because 'Luke had many trustworthy accounts to work from, and no portrayal of Paul can do without them', argues one German scholar.[7]

From the late nineteenth century, study on the historical Jesus attracted a wide field of academic disciplines. Ernst Renan and David Strauss wrote lives of Jesus, which astounded the Christian world by their application of critical analysis of the life of a Jewish prophet, who for most Christians was held to be a trans-historical figure. In 1907, Albert Schweitzer wrote a seminal analysis (*The Quest for the Historical Jesus*) that differentiated the historical figure of Jesus from the 'Christ' of Christian faith. Three *Quests* of Jesus have since then occurred, and North American scholars have led the field in contemporary studies. The major principles of historiography (scientific analysis of early source material) have recently been applied in a *Quest* to find the historical Paul.

Authorship of the Pauline Letters

Since the letters of Paul comprise the major part of the New Testament, his prominence in the early Christian movement cannot be disregarded. No understanding of Paul can be complete without resolving the issue of which of the thirteen letters attributed to Paul in the New Testament are authentic. With the exception of the letter to the Romans, Paul's letters were not treatises on theology, but were responses to problems arising in his communities. Paul was more a teacher than an author, and he wasn't the only missionary of the early decades: he had no role in the mission to preach the Gospel of Christ to pagan citizens in Egypt or Rome.

Most Christians are reasonably familiar with the term 'Gospel' (literally, the 'good news'), but what was the Radical Gospel of Paul? What was the message Paul delivered to Gentile citizens of the Roman Empire? Jesus of Nazareth preached the good news to Jewish peasants of Palestine: he was an itinerant prophet of the Kingdom of God who visited the local villages and hamlets of rural Galilee, but avoided the Greek metropolitan cities of Galilee and Judea (with the exception of Jerusalem and Jericho): there are no source traditions of Jesus entering Tiberias, Sepphoris, Scythopolis or Caesarea. This wasn't the case for Paul: he preached the Gospel of Christ crucified and risen in the major Greco-Roman cities and towns of Turkey,

Greece and Macedonia. The Jewish followers of Jesus had been Galilean fishermen of Capernaum, but Paul had once been a rabbinic scholar, and a Pharisee, the sect of which Jesus was critical (according to the Gospels). The contrast couldn't be starker.[A] Can we be sure the historical Jesus and the apostle Paul delivered the same message? And how was the Radical Gospel of Paul *initially heard* and *received* by Greco-Roman citizens? These questions are the focus of our study.

Some years ago I read a book on Paul by Günter Bornkamm. Bornkamm drew my attention to the significance of the collection that Paul arranged for the 'Saints of Jerusalem'.[B] Bornkamm showed that it was not merely a charitable deed, but was Paul's way of preserving unity within the Jesus community against a tide of ethnic prejudice prevalent in Jewish culture. He was trying to avoid a schism within Jewish and Gentile Christianity. Michael Goulder's book, *A Tale of Two Missions*, demonstrated more than Bornkamm had done the trials within the Jewish and Gentile assemblies: the tensions between Paul and James (and Cephas) in the first decades of the Jesus movement.[8] Paul became persona non-grata in Jerusalem at the end of his life. What these critical studies emphasised was a need to place Paul within the cultural tensions prevalent in first-century Judaism.

Jonathan Reed reveals the archaeology of some of the Jewish Settlements of the Mediterranean cities to show how widespread Jewish occupation had become in the Roman period of the early first century. John Crossan explores the coherence of Paul's Gospel with Roman Emperor worship. Bart Ehrman summarises the critical scholarship of the Pauline corpus, and looks at the exponential rise of conversion rates to Christianity in the first three centuries of the Roman Empire, and Tom Wright has recently written a biography of Paul's life and mission.[9]

I have depended on those authorities of Greco-Roman culture in the first-century world of the Roman Empire where Paul preached the Gospel of a crucified and resurrected Jewish Messiah, but there are others of a more

---

[A] Philippians 3:5
[B] Galatians 2:10; Romans 15:31–32; 1 Corinthians 16:1–4; 2 Corinthians 8 (18–21); Acts 2:41–47, 4:33–37.

conservative persuasion who take a less radical position on the Gospel of Paul than those who have informed my outlook. For those who find my treatment disturbing to the sensibilities of their faith, this study may not, perhaps, be best suited, but I aim to confront the credibility problems of Christian faith today in relation to the thought and person of Paul.

Structure of the Book

The first two chapters provide a context of the beginnings of the Roman Empire through to Constantine's reign. We examine the possible factors accounting for the success of the Christian mission, why the numbers of converts increased so rapidly, and what it was about Paul that made him such an effective missionary. We enquire whether the Christian teaching of Jesus as the Messianic Son of God was incidental to Caesar Augustus being addressed with the same titles. We move on to consider the themes of Paul's Radical Gospel in resect of three different presentations of him in the New Testament. Controversial claims are made of the authenticity of five letters traditionally ascribed to Paul have to be substantiated, and this is taken up in the closing chapters. A proposal to devise a renewed theology of Christian Scripture in the last chapter concludes the study.

I need to explain a few terms for the lay reader. When writing about the early followers of Jesus, I seldom use the term 'Church', but prefer to use *Jesus movement*. Scholars have used other descriptions, such as 'primitive Christianity', but whatever label is applied there's a recognition that the early community consisted of Jewish and Hellenistic Christians (the New Testament represents the beliefs of Hellenistic Christianity). This avoids the impression of the Jesus followers of the first decades being viewed as an organised and structured community (as the Church or a church). The early communities that Paul founded in Turkey, Greece and Macedonia were known as *ecclesias* (*ecclesia* was not so much a religious description, as a Greek term for 'a group of people with a common interest').

I occasionally use the word *Parousia*, which is Greek for the 'arrival of the person'. This term is found in the Greek New Testament for the second coming of Jesus. Other technical terms are explained in the text. Defining the Jewish God of Israel is complex. The Hebrew Bible has two titles for

God: *Elohim* (plural and singular) is translated as God, or the gods, and *Yahweh* as the Lord (both terms arising from Hebrew traditions collected after the Babylonian Exile). The title that Christians applied to Jesus was *Kyrios*, a Greek term meaning Lord or lord etc. The Jewish name for Jesus (*Iēsous*) means Saviour or Deliverer etc., and the term Christ (*Christos*) is a Greek equivalent for the Hebrew *Messiah*, which means King, Sovereign, or Monarch. The whole title of *Kyrios Iēsous Christos* translates as the Lord and Saviour, the King.

Notes

[1] 'Saul' is a Jewish name, after the first king of Israel: *Paulus or* 'Paul', as he is best known is the Latin equivalent.

[2] When Paul enumerates his Jewish credentials and writes 'a persecutor of the church', this is not to be read as a self-criticism, but rather as a boast. By persecuting the early Jesus community he was illustrating his zeal to be rid of apostate Jews (Philippians 3:5; 2 Corinthians 11:22; Romans 11:1).

[3] Bornkamm 1971: 3-12.

[4] High numbers of diaspora Jews settling in the Roman Empire are confirmed in Christian sources (Romans 2:17-24), Jewish sources (Philo: *De Vita Mosis* II: 20; Josephus: *Against Apian*) and Greco-Roman sources (Tacitus: *Annal XV* 44; Pliny the Younger: *Epistles X* 96). Philo confirms that the laws of the Jewish people had won the attention of barbarians, of Greeks, and of dwellers of the mainland and islands: Bornkamm 1971: 7.

[5] Bornkamm 1971: xx.

[6] Bornkamm 1971: x.

[7] Bornkamm 1971: xix.

[8] Goulder's book (2009) drew on the thesis of Ferdinand Baur in 1831.

[9] Crossan and Reed 2005, Crossan 1998, 2008, Ehrman 2018, and Wright 2018.

1

Caesar Augustus: Saviour of the World

The Battle at Actium

The Roman Empire experienced Civil War for over twenty years, and the whole Mediterranean world was in meltdown. Cassius and Brutus had assassinated Julius Caesar in 44 BCE, and his adopted son (Octavian) and general (Mark Antony) pursued his two assassins towards Philippi. The Republican system made up of the Senate and competing proconsuls was in conflict. Octavian was warding off rebellion to the west, and Antony had been plundering eastern lands to Parthia. At times they collaborated, at others times they were rivals, especially after Antony made a romantic alliance with Queen Cleopatra of Egypt (Cleopatra was a former mistress of Julius Caesar, the mother of Caesarion, Julius Caesar's natural son).

Mark Antony and Octavian Caesar were co-regents of the Roman Empire after the assassination of Julius Caesar; their struggle for power increased through the passing years. Then came the day when the rivalry would be settled. On 2 September 31 BCE, at Cape Actium, north-western Greece, the fleets of Antony and Cleopatra were trapped in the Ambracian Gulf. The summer had been exceptionally warm, supplies and resources were scarce, and Antony's men became ill with fever from mosquitoes. Morale was low and some began to defect to Octavian.

Octavian's military general was Marcus Agrippa and their fleet of ships were anchored in the Ionian Sea, thereby closing the mouth of the Gulf. Agrippa was a brilliant architect and admiral general. His smaller vessels were more manoeuvrable, and each had the deadly bronze battering ram with the *harpax*—a four-pronged iron hook to draw a vessel into the ram.

When the westerly winds blew south, the ships of Antony and Cleopatra came out of the Gulf and suffered losses. They were out manoeuvred by the strategic planning of Agrippa, but not before the ships of Antony and Cleopatra had escaped to Egypt. And when Octavian pursued them two years later he found they had both committed suicide. He paid Antony's troops well for their defection and loyalty, and they called out: 'Augustus [the venerated one], Saviour of Rome.'

Civil war in Rome came to an end on 1 August 30 BCE.

The Battle of Actium, 2 September 31 BC, Castro Lorenzo, 1664–1700

Caesar Augustus: the Son of God

Octavian could hardly believe his good fortune. Whilst asleep aboard his ship, Apollo appeared in a night-time vision and proclaimed him *Saviour of the world*, conqueror of sea and land. Julius Caesar also appeared in a vision and confirmed Octavian in the words: 'You are of my blood.'

Octavian built a monument on his campsite at Cape Actium (Nicopolis) in memory of his victory. Thirty battering rams from the fleets of Antony and Cleopatra were at the entrance, two tons of solid bronze apiece, with an inscription dedicated to Mars and Neptune (the gods of War and Sea) in gratitude for his victory at Actium. The inscription read:

> The Emperor Caesar, son of the Divine, victor in the war he waged on behalf of the Republic in this region, when he was consul for the fifth time and imperator for the seventh, after peace has been secured on

land and sea, consecrated to Mars (Ares) and Neptune (Poseidon) the camp from which he set to battle, adorned with naval spoils.[1]

Octavian was going forth to destiny. He made a move for Rome and was soon to become the *Imperator* (Emperor of Rome). He built a temple and dedicated it to Apollo on the Palatine Hill. Octavian would be recognised by the Senate as the Son of God, son of the divine Julius Caesar. So began the golden age of the Empire, an empire that was to last for 400 years.[2]

The monument at Cape Actium

After dispatching of Mark Antony and Cleopatra, Augustus stayed for a brief period in Alexandria. Unlike his predecessors, Augustus was not a looter so much as a tourist. He went to the tomb of Alexander the Great, whose body lay in state, embalmed in a coffin ornately decorated in gold and crystal, in accordance with Egyptian ritual.

Alexander the Great conquered the known world at 33 but Augustus had already turned 33 when disposing of Mark Antony, and all he managed to achieve was to unite the eastern and western provinces of the Empire. When asked to see the body of Alexander:

> The young Roman gazed at the body for a time; then paid his respects by crowning the head with a golden diadem and strewing flowers on the trunk. He was asked: 'Would you now like to visit the Mausoleum of the Ptolemies?' To which he retorted, 'I came to see a king, not a row of corpses'.[3]

Undoubtedly, Caesar Augustus admired Alexander greatly. He emulated him by creating an empire stretching from northern Spain to Armenia.

Octavian minted several silver denarii (a denarius was a labourer's daily pay) stamped with his own image and those of the deities of his imperial theology. Inscriptions referred to the deities:

Victoria—meaning Victory (Greek: Nike).

Venus—meaning Protection (Greek: Aphrodite)

Pax—meaning Peace (Greek: Eirene)

Coins were engraved with DVIF (*Divi Filius*), the 'Divine Son', or 'Son of the Divine' (Julius Caesar), the title given to Octavian Caesar Augustus.

Roman coins minted in honour of Caesar Augustus

Caesar Augustus was a human being who was believed to be divine and who was held to have gone to heaven. Throughout the Empire, including the provinces of Galilee and Judea, lords and commoners were regularly reminded of the stamp of Roman imperialism and the divinity of Caesar Augustus, divine Son of God. The title *Augustus* was engraved on coins and gates, road signs, aqueducts, bathhouses, palaces and amphitheatres: three were built in Palestine (at Sepphoris, Tiberias and Caesarea).

Amphitheatre and Roman Mosaics at Sepphoris in Galilee

Amphitheatres at Caesarea Maritima and Scythopolis in Judea

Pagan Religion

'Paganism' was a slogan coined by early Christians for anyone who was neither Jewish nor Christian.[4] Greco-Roman citizens would not have seen themselves as *pagans*. First-century Romans were incredibly superstitious by nature and religious ritual influenced every facet of their cultural life; it was practised by both lords and peasants alike. Religion was not about what a Greco-Roman believed, but about what s/he did: animal sacrifices were offered to popular gods unquestioningly for bountiful harvests, for promoting good health, or for invoking blessings before going into battle.

Worship rarely involved the whole community in a collective ceremony, apart from the annual festivals, but was a private familial affair. Romans were not so much polytheists as *henotheists* (devotees of a favoured god), but many educated and enlightened Greco-Romans thought there was an overseeing deity, a Supreme Being over the cosmos, which they knew to be *Theos Hypsistos*.[5]

Emperor Worship

There were civic cults, family cults and the imperial cults, many of which involved Romans praying and offering animal sacrifices and food gifts of placation. Worshippers in the provinces honoured the imperial emperors after their deaths, and anniversaries marked the occasion of a festival:

> We have a calendar of festivals observed by the Roman army from the third century CE that indicates that anniversaries of deified emperors were to be observed through sacrifices, whereas anniversaries of the current emperor were marked either by offerings to his genius or an offering to other divinities connected with his rule, such as the trio of divinities associated with the Capitoline Hill in Rome: Jupiter, Juno (his wife), and Minerva'.[6]

An inscription has been found in a town near Sparta, Greece that recalls a festival on one particular day for 'the god Caesar Augustus, Son of God, our Saviour and Deliverer' and on the next day for the 'Emperor Tiberius Caesar Augustus, father of the fatherland.'[7]

Julius Caesar publicly proclaimed his family had descended from Venus, and Caesar Augustus also promoted his divine status. But the Senate did not declare every emperor divine at death: those behaving outrageously or immorally, such as Nero and Caligula, were not granted divine status (Nero promoted his own divinity whilst in office).

Worship of the deceased emperors was a foundation of Roman imperial theology, a theology which acknowledged the role of religion in bringing victory (Augustus prayed and offered sacrifices to the gods before going into battle): it was the guiding principle for peace in Rome (*Pax Romana*).

'Octavian Caesar Augustus' (Greek: σεβαστοι)

What would happen, then, when the lofty titles were transferred from an Emperor of the Palatine hills of Rome to a Jewish prophet of an unknown village in the province of Galilee? It would have been treason in the first century to honour an alternative Lord to Caesar. Augustus was respected as Lord and Saviour of the Empire, but for a Jewish missionary of Christ, Jesus was the Lord (the *Kyrios*) and *Saviour* of the world, the Son of God, who, within three centuries, would be thought of as God incarnate (God of God). The Radical Gospel of Paul only required Roman citizens to:

> Confess with your mouth *Jesus as Lord* and believe in your heart that God has raised him from the dead [and] you will be saved.[A]

This was the religio-political context of the Roman Empire during the 40s and 50s of the first century in which Paul delivered the Radical Gospel of Christ crucified and risen, the eternal Saviour of the world.

Notes

[1] Hölscher 2006: https://landscapeandmemoryintheancientworld.wordpress.com/2017/10/17/octavians-victory-monument-at-nicopolis-a-symbol-of-status-quo/

[2] Adapted lecture given by John Dominic Crossan: viewable on YouTube: https://www.youtube.com/watch?v=ZJiPpAnFe4A.

[3] Everitt 2007.

[4] The definition of paganism derives from the Latin term *paganus*, which refers to one who resides in the countryside, the inference being that only country bumpkins continue to observe the backward customs of ignorant ancestors. Christians used the term to denigrate non-Christians: Ehrman 2018: 77.

[5] This didn't mean that worshippers were monotheistic, as the term 'one' did not imply the exclusion of others. Comparable use of the term on inscriptions didn't imply singularity. Inscriptions on town walls and city gates often read the *one patriot and benefactor*: 'one patriot' didn't mean the exclusion of other benefactors, only that a particular person had donated more than all others to the city: Ehrman 2018: 114.

[6] *Sol Invictus*: the Unconquered Sun was also worshipped widely in Rome.

[7] Ehrman 2018: 101.

[A] Romans 10:9

2

Constantine Becomes a Christian

Why did Christianity become such a successful religion of the Empire? It is sometimes thought that Christianity triumphed after the conversion of Constantine in 312 CE, but research has shown that numbers would have grown in spite of the conversion of Constantine. Did the successes of the Christian mission have anything to do with succeeding political changes in Roman governance, then? It is also believed that conversions increased *because of persecution*, that martyrdom accounted for a paradoxical rise in Christian membership. Although skirmishes and tribulation occurred in a few places, wide-scale persecution by Roman Emperors was infrequent. We examine the limited data available on the effects of the conversion of Constantine, the rise in conversion rates to the Church, and the degree of Christian persecution from the first to the fourth century.

The Conversion of Constantine

Constantine was converted on 27 October 312 CE. Some historians have questioned whether his conversion was sincere, but according to his own testimony and the accounts of his chroniclers, his conversion was sincere. We may ask: *What actually changed?* Constantine switched his allegiances from one set of religious beliefs and practices to another.[1] He was raised a polytheist who worshipped the deities of his family, his home (Naissus, in Serbia), his army and the deities of the pantheon, depending on where he may have settled, but everything changed at the Battle of the Milvian Bridge, when he was reported to have experienced a vision of the Cross of Christ with two Greek letters: *Chi* and *Ro* (an abbreviation for 'Christ').

Battle of Milvian Bridge, Pieter Lastman, 1613

Most people (93%) in the Roman Empire were polytheists or henotheists, and so conversion had no real significance, but when pagans converted to Christianity they were expected to become monotheists and worship only the God of Jesus: Christianity was an *exclusive religion*. From the first Commandment of Moses—'You shall worship *no other god*; for the Lord, whose name is *Jealous*, is a *jealous* God'—Paul reminds the Thessalonians of what they had left behind when becoming Christians.[A] He wrote:

[A] Exodus 34:14 (20:5)

> The people of those regions report about us what kind of welcome we had among you, and how *you turned to God from idols*, to serve a living and true God.[A]

When pagan citizens became Christians, they were no longer to worship the gods of their ancestors. In the pagan world of the early first century, everyone was religious: it was the cultural norm. When new deities were introduced to the populous, they would enter the pantheon. The Romans accepted the gods of other nations, and so there were equivalent gods for the Greek gods Zeus (Jupiter) and Aphrodite (Venus), but it never meant that a Greco-Roman would end his or her allegiance to their popular god. When a pagan converted to Christianity, however, it was not the same. A convert to the Church was not permitted to practise pagan *and* Christian worship. Because early Christians ceased to be polytheists and refused to take part in imperial ceremonies and Emperor worship, they were often regarded by the populous as atheists.

Temple Ruins of Aphrodite (Venus: Rome) in Aphrodisias (Turkey)

[A] 1 Thessalonians 1:9

Expansion of Christian Numbers under Constantine

Constantine never enforced Christianity as the only permitted religion of Rome, but by 300 CE there were between four and six million Christians in the Roman Empire, and at the end of the next century there were thirty million Christians in the Empire.

Adolf von Harnack said that 7% to 10% of the population of the Empire had become Christian by the beginning of the fourth century, and that:

> By the end of the fourth century, it is typically maintained, something like half of the empire's sixty million inhabitants claimed allegiance to the Christian tradition.[2]

Constantine was declared Emperor of the Roman Empire at York in 306.

We find evidence of early Christian expansion in Acts. After Peter gave a sermon in Jerusalem, 3,000 persons were baptised in just a day; a further

5,000 joined the movement when he and John preached in the Temple. And later on:

> More than ever believers were added to the Lord, *great numbers* of both men and women, so that they even carried out the sick into the streets, and laid them on cots and mats, in order that Peter's shadow might fall on some of them as he came by. A *great number* of people would also gather from the towns around Jerusalem, bringing the sick and those tormented by unclean spirits, and they were *all cured*.[A]

Such high numbers in ancient sources are not dependable, however, as at this rate, writes Ehrman, the whole Empire would have become Christian by 50 CE.[3] It might be that many early converts in Jerusalem were latent followers of the historical Jesus, though we have no way of knowing this.

Historical Data on Christian Expansion

Two historical facts emerge from the data. Eusebius cites a Roman bishop in the mid-third century named Cornelius, who compiled a report of the number of helpers serving in his church.[B] He says there were at the time:

> 46 presbyters, 7 deacons, 4 sub-deacons, 42 acolytes,
> 52 exorcists, readers and doorkeepers, and
> 1,500 widows and other persons requiring some support.

Counting the bishop, his church had 155 clergy giving charitable support for 1,500 in a city of one million. From such data alone, Harnack surmises that his church in Rome must have had approximately 30,000 members, and adds that his estimation may be too low. John Chrysostom, a bishop of Constantinople during the fourth century, wrote about his community of 100,000 Christians offering material support for 3,000 needy members (3% of the population of Constantinople). Ehrman concludes that:

[A] Acts 2:41, 4:4, 5:14
[B] Eusebius, *Church History* 6.43

If a comparable rate applied to the church in Rome some decades earlier, the church may have numbered something like 50,000, comprising 5% of the population of the city at the time.[4]

This is the mathematical miracle of the exponential curve. There begins a slow rate of growth that increases at a considerable rate by the end of the period. The Church would only have to grow by three to four converts in every hundred, in each decade, to reach thirty million by 400 CE (below a breakdown is provided). Consider the evidence of Christian expansion in the New Testament.

Christian Communities
Number of Converts

We can observe the numbers of members in Paul's *ecclesias* through some incidental details provided in his letters. They consisted of quite a mixed bunch of converts. Roman citizens joining the Christian fellowships rose increasingly in the first three decades of preaching the Gospel. The first letter Paul wrote to the Thessalonians was addressed to an *ecclesia* where some had died before the advent of Jesus at the *Parousia*: the community could not have been small in number.

In his first letter to the Corinthians, Paul is critical about schisms in the fellowship: some believers boasted about speaking in the voices of angels and others about healing, some had advanced new and radical teachings, and others had become conservative, some had been gorging themselves, whilst others went hungry, some had been buying sacrificial meat at the market beyond reproach, whilst others were anxious about worshipping Christ with heads unveiled. The *ecclesia* at Corinth couldn't have been an insignificant community, but one having thirty to sixty members.

The letter to the Romans (an *ecclesia* not established, or even visited by Paul) cites 27 principal members by name, and there were *ecclesias* in the cities of Jerusalem, Damascus and Antioch not founded by Paul. From incidental evidence in the New Testament writings of Paul, we see that a considerable following existed within thirty years of the Jesus movement.

Demographic of the Post-Apostolic Churches

One pagan author was outspokenly cynical about Christians. Celsus was an intellectual of Rome who delighted in mocking Christianity:

> Wherever one finds a crowd of adolescent boys, or a bunch of slaves, or a company of fools, there will Christian teachers be also, showing off their fine new philosophy. In private houses one can see wool workers, cobblers, laundry workers, and the most illiterate country bumpkins, who would not venture to voice their opinions in front of their intellectual betters. But let them get hold of children in private houses—let them find some gullible wives—and you will hear some preposterous statements. You will hear them say, for instance, that they should not pay any attention to their fathers or teachers, but must obey them. They say that their elders and teachers are fools, and are in reality very bad men who like to voice their silly opinions…
>
> Now if, as they are speaking thus to the children, they happen to see a schoolteacher coming along, some intelligent person, or even the father of one of the children, these Christians flee in all directions….
>
> These Christians also tell the children that they should leave their fathers and teachers and follow the women and the little chums to the wool dresser's shop, or the cobbler's or the washer woman's shop, so they might learn how to be perfect. And by this logic they have persuaded many to join them.[5]

Such a critique is confirmed by Paul in his first letter to the Corinthians, where he reminds converts to:

> Consider your own call, brothers and sisters: *not many of you were wise by human standards, not many were powerful, not many were of noble birth.*[A]

In spite of ridiculing Christian teachers and impressionable youngsters as Celsus did, Paul confirmed that many converts were uneducated. But he pointed to this as evidence that God's selection was to *confound the wise*.

[A] 1 Corinthians 1:26–27

Origen said something similar in his day. Celsus also slurred Christianity as attracting more women than men, and this can also be confirmed by a report of personal belongings confiscated from members of one church in North Africa when Diocletian inaugurated his world-wide persecution of Christians in 303 CE: personal items included 16 men's tunics against 82 women's tunics, 38 veils and 47 pairs of female slippers. Robin Lane Fox correctly observes:

> It is highly likely that women were a clear majority in the churches of the third century'.[6]

Social Advance of Christianity

Luke records Simon Peter as the leading apostle (confirmed also by Paul) in the Jewish mission. We have no authentic documents written by any of the twelve disciples of Jesus to carry out an assessment of their literary abilities. Scholars have doubts about whether any of the disciples were as articulate as Luke suggests about Simon Peter in Acts (we know so little about them, and archaeological and anthropological studies have shown that first-century peasants were unable to write documents: Chapter 8).

However, within a brief period, educated scholars amongst the Jewish community in Judea and beyond (i.e. Paul and Apollos) entered the Jesus movement who knew the Scriptures sufficiently to convince their Jewish contemporaries that Jesus had been the promised Messiah. The notion of an executed messiah-deliverer was probably not figured out by Paul, but by latent followers of Jesus amongst the Jewish rabbis in Judea who came out of the woodwork after the resurrection.

Galilean peasants couldn't afford a formal education, and most pagans in the empire were poor and illiterate, but there were scholars and scribes in Judea, and certainly of the diaspora amongst the Mediterranean cities. Besides the four evangelists, there were prominent teachers in a number of *ecclesias* cited by name in Paul's closing benedictions. Then we think of the early Christian bishops and writers, Justin Martyr, Irenaeus, Ignatius, Origen, Tertullian, Eusebius, Ambrose and Augustine, who were able to articulate the message, and who could engage in philosophical discourse and rhetoric up to and beyond Nicaea. Even in modern times, educated writers, poets, artists and philosophers have been inspired and informed by Christian motifs. Without Christianity:

> We would never have had the Middle Ages, the Reformation, the Renaissance or modernity as we know it. And there could never have been a Matthew Arnold. Or any of the Victorian poets. Or any of the other authors of our literary canon: no Milton, no Shakespeare, no Chaucer. We would have had none of our revered artists: Michelangelo, Leonardo da Vinci, or Rembrandt. And none of our brilliant composers: Mozart, Handel, or Bach.[7]

Did Persecution Foster Christian Expansion?

We have a first-hand account of Paul's sufferings:

> Are they descendants of Abraham? So am I. Are they ministers of Christ? I am talking like a madman—I am a better one: with far greater labours, far more imprisonments, with countless floggings, and often near death. *Five times* I have received from the Jews the *forty lashes minus one*. *Three times* I was *beaten with rods*. *Once* I received a *stoning*. Three times I was shipwrecked; for a night and a day I was adrift at sea; on frequent journeys, in danger from rivers, danger from bandits, danger from my own people, danger from Gentiles, danger in the city, danger in the wilderness, danger at sea, danger from false brothers and sisters; in toil and hardship, through many a sleepless night, hungry and thirsty, often without food, cold and naked. And, besides other things, I am under daily pressure because of my anxiety for all the churches.[8]

The list of Jewish beatings is not traceable in Acts. Recorded persecutions include the stoning of Stephen and the death of James by Agrippa. Other sources record the executions of Peter and Paul, the persecutions by Nero in Rome, and Pliny the Younger in Pontus and Bithynia, the beheading of Justin Martyr in Rome, and the martyrdom of Polycarp in Smyrna.

However, political persecution of Christians by the Roman State was rare and isolated, often sporadic (occurring in 250, 257-258 and 303-313 CE). There were local beatings by Jews on their fellows, as Paul experienced, and a few political trials in Rome, but the notion of perennial persecution of Christianity as an illicit religion under constant surveillance by a State apparatus inflicting martyrdom on countless believers and forcing them underground in Roman catacombs remains the story of legend.

We are not saying there weren't some ghastly incidents on occasions that involved bringing believers to trial, torchers and horrific executions, but the only imperial persecution occurred under Diocletian during the third century (303 CE).[9] Small-scale persecution never deterred the endeavours of the early Christian missionaries, and neither did it stem the steady tide of pagans joining the Church, but a direct correlation between Christian persecution and risen numbers has not been demonstrated. However, the political influences of the administration—the conversion of Constantine and the procurement of Christianity by Theodosius II—have been shown to be positive factors of rising conversion rates in the early fifth century. Consider the uncompromising Theodosian Codes (*Codex Theodosianus*) in 429 CE condemning paganism, as examples of anti-paganism:

> All heretics of every type–that is, anyone not subscribing to the creed of Nicaea–were forbidden to have any meeting places [and] were to be expelled from the cities and driven forth from the villages...
>
> They were to be sought out in all places and forced to return to their countries of origin. Anyone who did not subscribe to the 'apostolic discipline and the evangelical doctrine' that promoted the theologically correct understanding of the Trinity....
>
> [Anyone who] was legally pronounced 'demented and insane' was to be 'smitten first by divine vengeance and secondly by the retribution of Our own initiative, which We shall assume in accordance with the divine judgement.'[A]

How Christians Won Converts

On two occasions Luke recalls a typical pattern of Christian conversion. When a young woman of Lydia and a jailer at Philippi both converted to Christianity they brought along their *entire* family to be baptised into the Church.[10] There were no means of organising headcounts of Christians in

---

[A] *Codex Theodosianus* 16.1.2, 5–20

the ancient world. Luke's reports of the exceptionally high numbers of conversions have to be regarded as generalisations (exaggerations), but if individual conversions implied the conversions of one's whole family we can see how numbers would rise.

We are not to imagine, Ehrman argues, crusades and open-tent meetings to evangelise the populace, or the forms of Christian pioneering to bring Christ to new continents, as occurred in the 18th century. The consensus of opinion amongst Christian historians is that a steady rise in conversion rates occurred through word-of-mouth conversations, social networking and commerce. A converted Christian might discuss with a fellow trader a newfound belief in Jesus, and he, in turn, brings along his whole family and, say, his partner talks about Jesus to her friends washing garments in the river, and so on, to such an extent that small groups of Christians form, which grow and join into a larger community to become an *ecclesia* (i.e. a small group worshipping Jesus in the house of a wealthy believer).

Sylvester receiving the donation from Emperor Constantine: School of Raphael, commissioned by Pope Leo X in 1517

Why Christian Numbers Grew under Constantine

There were social attractions and financial benefits for wealthier converts to Christianity after Constantine converted. Status, positions and favours were offered to elites who toed the party line with Constantine, but even for poorer citizens there were benefits. Pagan practices involved people sacrificing to gods in exchange for divine blessings on an *individual basis,* whilst the Christian *ecclesias* offered converts a *sense of community*—as the Jews experienced in synagogues every Sabbath—in religious ceremonies on a weekly basis. Material support and food were also given to widows and poorer believers. Christian stories of miracles gave rise to a sense of omnipotent power over the natural elements, and legends of miraculous conversions and supernatural martyrdoms were a source of inspiration. The hope of being saved from the dreadful imaginations of an afterlife of perpetual torment would have provided a sense of solace and comfort, a point to which we shall return.

Summary

The population of the Empire abandoned paganism for Christianity by the close of the fourth century (from sixty million citizens, thirty million had converted to Christianity). Congregation numbers exploded after the conversion of Constantine, and under his reign Christianity became the most popular and profitable religion to practice.

Constantine's conversion was not the only catalyst for growing Christian numbers. Historians have shown that conversion rates of Christians had been steadily and consistently rising before the reign of Constantine, and that the Church would have expanded even if he'd never converted from paganism. Two growth spurts in conversion rates occurred from the first to the fourth century: a) the first two decades, and b) after Constantine's conversion. On sociological grounds alone, we can account for the latter, but for the early period we turn to Paul.

Notes

[1] Constantine had watched and may have been complicit in the persecution of Christians under Diocletian and Galerius (Eusebius *Church History* 8, 17), his general, until his father died in 311 CE when he became Augustus. The Edict of Milan by Constantine and Lucinius in 311 was the first official Code to grant tolerance and freedom of Christianity *and* pagan religion.

Towards the end of the fourth century, an increasingly cruel streak arose in the treatment of slaves when Constantine became Christian. The Theodosian Code (9. 5. 1.1) states that 'slaves who informed on their masters were to be crucified'. In 237, Constantine not only had his nephew, the son of his rival, Galerius, executed, but ordered the deaths of his eldest son Crispus and his wife Faustus: Crispus was murdered or executed, his mother was cooked to death in an overheated steam bath. Constantine's predecessors were viewed to be chief priests, *Pontifex Maximus*, of the religions of Rome. Religion and State were intertwined, and every emperor following Constantine (with the exception of his nephew Julian, who reigned for a brief time) was a Christian. It is therefore incorrect to assume that Constantine, in place of Theodosian, declared Christianity as the official religion of the Empire: Ehrman 2018: 239.

Constantine allegedly wrote a document called the Donation, which declared that he had authorised that Rome and the western provinces be in possession of the bishop of the city. This was shown to be a forgery in the mid-fifteenth century. A thirteenth century Pope (Gregory IX 1227–1241) used it to confront Frederick II, King of Sicily and claimed that Constantine gave the Bishop of Rome the imperial insignia and sceptre. Pope Boniface VIII (1294–1303) said: 'I am Caesar; I am the Emperor': Ehrman 2018: 284.

[2] Harnack 1908: 248; Ehrman 2018: 105.

[3] Ehrman 2018: 162.

[4] Ehrman 2018: 164–165.

[5] Ehrman 2018: 132–133.

[6] Quoted in Ehrman 2018: 134.

[7] Ehrman 2018: 4.

[8] 2 Corinthians 11:22–28: Jewish discipline was endorsed in Deuteronomy 25:3:

> Suppose two persons have a dispute and enter into litigation, and the judges decide between them, declaring one to be in the right and the other to be in the wrong. If the one in the wrong deserves to be flogged, the judge shall make that person lie down and be beaten in his presence with the number of lashes proportionate to the offense. Forty lashes may be given but not more; if more lashes than these are given, your neighbour…

[9] Diocletian (284–305) was a pagan emperor who viewed Christian 'atheism' as a threat to the Empire. He issued a first edict on 2 February 303 CE, in which he declared all Christian meetings illegal. Christian places of worship were to be destroyed, the Christian Scriptures were to be confiscated, those of social status were to lose their rank, and Christian freedmen in imperial service were to be re-enslaved. Apart from Christian buildings being destroyed by marauding monks, the edict had little effect. There were no municipal police to carry out the decree. Further decrees were issued to arrest the clergy, and a final edict in the spring of 304 required everyone in the Empire to gather in public places and participate in sacrifices. This came to a timely end with the Edict of Milan in 313 by Constantine and his co-emperor Lucinius.

[10] Philippi was the Roman city where Octavian and Mark Anthony defeated Brutus and Cassius for assassinating Julius Caesar: Wright 2018: 178.

Estimations of Growth in Christian Numbers (Ehrman 2018: 171)

30 CE	20	250 CE	600,000–700,000
60 CE	1,000–1,500	300 CE	2.5–3.5 million
100 CE	7,000–10,000	312 CE	3.5–4 million
150 CE	30,000–40,000	400 CE	25–35 million
200 CE	140,000–170,000		

3

A Tale of Two Saviours

The Mazeus-Mithridates Gate in Ephesus

Review: Caesar Augustus the Saviour of the world

Rome had found her Saviour in Octavian after the twenty-year Civil War ended. Octavian had been proclaimed *princeps senatus* (principal member of the Senate) and *Imperator* (Emperor), and the Senate could rest. Caesar Augustus became the most effective emperor of the Empire, in grabbing new territory and patrolling the borders. He was announced *divine* by the Senate at death and was believed to have *ascended to heaven*, like Jupiter, god of thunder. Poets and playwrights (Virgil, Horace, Ovid) portrayed Augustus as the *God of gods*, and a festival was held in his honour.

Imperial theology became the catalyst that held the Empire together, and the name of Augustus was publicised widely throughout his domain.

Inscription of the Divine Son of God Augustus

On the gate to the commercial Agora and the city Library (where lectures would be held) at Ephesus exists an inscription inlaid with bronze letters of the city's patrons in honour of Octavian Augustus Caesar, Son of God:

Imperator Caesar Divi Filius Augustus, Pontifex Maximus
(Emperor Caesar, Son of the Divine, Augustus, Greatest Priest).

If an itinerant missionary from Cilicia were to enter the city talking about another Saviour of the world, he'd better have a content that made sense to people. When Paul proclaimed 'Jesus is Lord' it would become a threat to the Roman Administration. In the Roman Empire of the first century, *it was high treason* to profess an alternative Lord to Lord Caesar.

Jesus Christ: Saviour of the world

What would Paul have felt when he walked through the gate at Ephesus, and other similar gates of the Mediterranean cities? Caesar Augustus met every need in food and security after the Civil War came to a close; what could Paul offer pagans with another Saviour of the world, **the only** Son of God? Paul's Lord needed to prove a more powerful Lord than Caesar Augustus, Tiberius and every future emperor could ever have been. The

Radical Gospel of Paul said that Jesus of Nazareth was the *Almighty* Lord and *Saviour* of the world. The challenge for the apostle was in promoting the new social and political order of an executed and resurrected Christ, who was to supersede every almighty Roman Emperor.[1]

There are seven letters that critical scholars consider are clearly authentic to Paul. Critics have pointed out that six of Paul's letters bear evidence of redaction by early Christian scribes who wished to bring Paul's teaching into line with what modern theologians term 'proto-orthodoxy', a topic we take up in Chapters 8-9. We consider below the social implications of Paul's Radical Gospel of Christ crucified.

The Radical Saul of Tarsus

There are three presentations of Paul in the New Testament. There is the **Radical Paul**, as presented in Paul's authentic letters; the **Liberal Paul**, as found in the letters to the Ephesians and Colossians, which some scholars believe were probably not written by Paul; and the **Conservative Paul**, as found in the so-called pastoral letters, 1 and 2 Timothy and Titus, three letters which the majority of critical scholars believe were not written by Paul. In summary, we have in the New Testament:

- The **Radical Paul** of Galatians, 1 & 2 Corinthians, Philippians, 1 Thessalonians, Philemon and Romans.[A]
- The **Liberal Paul** of Ephesians, Colossians and Acts.[B]
- The **Conservative Paul** of 2 Thessalonians, 1 and 2 Timothy, and Titus.[C]

Take gender as a case, according to the first letter to Timothy, women in the *ecclesias* had to dress modestly and be subordinate to men: they must *keep quiet* during worship and were *not permitted to teach* in the *ecclesias*. If they have a question, they were to wait until they got home and ask their husbands. The letter also suggests that women have to get pregnant to be

---

[A] Galatians 3:28–29, 1& 2 Corinthians, Philippians, 1 Thessalonians, Philemon 8–22; Romans 16:1–3, 7
[B] Ephesians 5:22–33, 6:5–9; Colossians 3:18–25, 4:1–2
[C] 1Timothy 6:1–2, Titus 2:3–5, 9–10

saved! The letter to the Ephesians was not quite so prescriptive. Christian wives were still expected to be subject to their husbands, but husbands had to love their wives, as Christ loved and gave himself for the Church. As Crossan remarks: 'I would go for that obedience option than have to give up my life, especially since the Church has never obeyed Christ!'[2]

The letter to the Romans was hand-delivered to the *ecclesias* in Rome by Phoebe and we get the impression that Paul made no distinction between men and women in the *ecclesias*.[3] He wasn't being a feminist, but would simply ask who was going to Rome, and Phoebe offered to take the letter. But she wouldn't just drop the letter into a mailbox of the Roman church; she would read the letter out loud in the *ecclesia*, clarify what Paul meant, and expound on anything not understood, which would've been difficult if women in the *ecclesias* had to be silent!

What was the practice in the *ecclesias* of Paul in terms of gender relations? It appears as though Christian women took as much a part in worship as did men, and that someone (Christian scribe) came along and attempted to *de-radicalise Paul, sanitise Paul, make him safe by adjusting his views* to suit the patriarchal Roman society.

The Gospel of Paul had social obligations that were to have an impact on the paterfamilias structure of Roman society, requirements that for Paul were implicit in the teaching of Jesus, demographic changes in respect of ethnicity, slavery and gender.

No Privileged Ethnicity in Christ

The social imperatives implicit in Paul's Radical Gospel that converts to Christ were to live by are succinctly stated in the letter to the Galatians:

> There is *no longer Jew or Greek, there is no longer slave or free, there is no longer male and female*; for all of you are one in Christ...[A]

Diaspora Jews were not a marginalised community hidden away in some

---

[A] Galatians 3:28–29

secret ghetto of the Roman Empire, but were a proud and distinguished people content within the provincial regions of the Mediterranean. In the ancient ruins of Aphrodisias, a nameplate from a gatepost (possibly from a Jewish synagogue) has been found bearing an inscription in recognition of the 126 donors who financed the building. Of these donors, 55% were Jews, 2% were pagan converts to Judaism (circumcised, if male) and 43% were pagans. The first nine were members of the city council (the *boulé*), but the first patron recorded was a woman, the only woman on the list.[4]

Ancient Runes of Aphrodisias (western Turkey)

If Jews had become well integrated within the provinces of Greco-Roman society, and pagan citizens not only accepted their contributions, but also attended local synagogues, we have a context for Luke's citing in Acts of the *God-fearers*, or the *God-worshippers*, drawing towards Judaism.[A] Could they have been Paul's target audience? Luke presented Paul going out to the *Jewish synagogues to convert the Jews*, but Paul declared of himself that God 'Set *me* apart before I was born... *to preach among the Gentiles.*'[B]

[A] Acts 10:22, 13:50, 17:4, 17, 1:7
[B] Galatians 1:15–16; Romans 11:13

It seems that Paul was going for the God-fearing pagans; he was 'convert poaching', in the words of Crossan.[5] The Jewish synagogues were where Paul would knowingly meet up with his fellow Jews of the diaspora, and where he could also reach out to those God-fearers attracted to Judaism, who weren't prepared to depart from the customs of their ancestors, to be circumcised and to adopt the kosher dietary regulations of the Torah. The Radical Gospel only required God-fearers to reject polytheism.

Judaism was not essentially a missionary religion. The Jews seldom tried to convert the pagans, but conversion occurs not only through coercion, but also by *attraction*. We have evidence in Christian and secular sources of pagans being attracted to Judaism. They attended local synagogues in major Roman cities: they admired their familial bonds of community and the imperatives of the Mosaic Law; the enlightened believed that Jewish monotheism was philosophically sound, but many pagans would never become fully Jewish and accept circumcision or practise kosher.[A]

Social upheaval and confrontation occurred between Paul and his Jewish folk for luring away the God-fearing adherents to Judaism. There were feuds and arguments of former neighbours against converted pagans for leaving the synagogues: Paul was persecuted by both parties (Jewish and pagan), because Christianity had morphed into an exclusive religion. The Radical Gospel of Paul required all converted pagans to reject polytheism and henotheism altogether, since Christian converts were not permitted to worship pagan gods *and* the God of the Christians.

The Jewish-pagan connections explain a number of historical anomalies:

- they explain how the Greco-Roman God-fearers would be able to make sense of Paul's analogies from Jewish Scripture, and
- they explain why they would care about the heritage of Judaism.

If Christian missionaries informed the God-fearers there was no longer a need to adopt the dietary codes of the Torah, or be circumcised, or keep the Sabbath for salvation, that all they were expected to do was to accept Jesus as Lord and Saviour, it would be appealing. All they were required

---

[A] Romans 1:18–31

to do was to convert to Christianity. If Paul was going for the in-between group, it would be a challenge for Romans to maintain peace and control. What Gospel could Paul offer citizens that could possibly compete with what Caesar Augustus had done for them? The Roman Emperor brought peace by *combat* and *military* victory. Jesus Christ was also to subdue the nations 'under his feet', but by means of *justice*.[6] Whilst many elites had prospered under the programme of Caesar Augustus, not every one had benefitted. Ehrman has addressed the political and religious factors that influenced the advance of Christianity in the three centuries from Jesus to Constantine.[7] Below we consider the social implications of Paul's Radical Gospel. What were the social changes for pagan converts to Christianity?

Paul said there was no longer a racial or ethnic barrier between Jews and Gentiles, because in Christ Jesus all are one: *all are children of God's family*. The credo recalled in Paul's letter to the Galatians was aimed at breaking down the racial and ethnic boundaries within Roman society. Paul said:

There is no longer Jew or Greek, for all of you are one in Christ Jesus.

No Slaves in Christ

'Slavery in Paul's world had nothing to do with ethnic origin… [Slavery] was complex but omnipresent.'[8] Life as a Roman slave in the first century was a miserable existence, particularly for soldiers on the losing side of a battle and for failed businessmen, who were forced to sell their labour to survive, but a few slaves were respected and some had risen to become a patron's right-hand man (as Tiro was, Cicero's slave). Slaves were often exploited, abused and treated harshly, and those in prison often caught a mortal disease and suffered from dysentery after drinking polluted water amongst rats and human faeces. Paul knew that the God of Israel was the *slave-liberating God*—it was the Exodus story. For the first-century slave to discover there is a God in heaven who had loved them and sacrificed his only Son for them would be an appealing message.[A]

Romans had different ways of treating runaway slaves. If one was caught

---

[A] Galatians 2:20

escaping from his master he would be crucified or punished severely, but if he had a justifiable complaint to run away he could seek redress from a senior patron to his *owner*. Romans had three forms of imprisonment:

- A low-status prisoner would be secured in a dungeon to rot.
- A higher-status prisoner would be chained in the guardhouse.
- The highest-status prisoner would be held under house arrest.

Paul had been arrested and was in a proconsul prison at Ephesus: he had a certain amount of freedom, since believers were coming and going. He was under house arrest but was still at risk of losing his life (it depended on a guard's goodwill or his openness to bribery). This is the background to Paul's letter to Philemon.

Onesimus had been a runaway slave *owned* by Philemon. How are we to understand his situation? As a runaway slave, he could be crucified if he was caught, but if he could reach a superior patron and appeal for mercy, he may get reprieved. A well-known case involved a servant accidentally breaking a crystal vase belonging to his patron, whereupon he was to be tossed into his pool of lamprey eels. Augustus witnessed the episode and considered his punishment far too severe. He counter-ordered that every crystal vase in the patron's house was to be broken and the lamprey eels destroyed.

Onesimus had escaped from Philemon and had managed to reach Paul in custody without being caught. Paul *pleads a* case for Onesimus. The letter illustrates the character and the theology of Paul. If he were to adopt the imperatives outlined in the letters to the Colossians and the Ephesians he would demand that Onesimus went back to his master, say he was sorry and be an obedient slave; and to Philemon he would ask him to go easy with Onesimus and not be too brutal. But he doesn't. He wants Philemon to know that Onesimus has converted to Christ, and that he is his brother in Christ, that Christian masters cannot *own* Christian slaves and remain 'in the Lord'. As Paul wrote in his letter to the Galatians:

> *There is no longer slave or free*, for all of you are one in Christ.[9]

Note what Paul does: he addresses the letter to Philemon *and* to everyone else in his house *ecclesia*; the letter was sent not only from Paul, but from his aids; it was intended to be read in public in Philemon's house *ecclesia*. The **Radical Paul** appeals to Philemon (note the earnestness of language):

> I am appealing to you for my child, Onesimus, whose father I have become during my imprisonment. Formerly he was useless to you, but now he is indeed useful both to you and to me. I am sending him, that is, my own heart, back to you... So if you consider me your partner, welcome him as you would welcome me. If he has wronged you in any way, or owes you anything, charge that to my account. I, Paul, am writing this with my own hand: I will repay it. I say nothing about your owing me even your own self. Yes, brother, let me have this benefit from you in the Lord! Refresh my heart in Christ. Confident of your obedience, I am writing to you, knowing that you will do even more than I say.[A]

Every phrase is loaded in the hope of Christian expectation for a convert who has accepted Christ. Paul yearns for *his own child* (Onesimus), for his *own heart*; he specifies his value to both of them and offers to *pay his debts*, to *charge that to his account*. He is prompted to recall what was personally owed to Paul: namely, his salvation (Paul probably converted Philemon). He implies that he knows he *will comply and agree to put things right* ('even more than I say'), but, note, he doesn't 'order him'. Paul further implies it was God's will for this to have happened. I can't imagine Philemon could have refused to have Onesimus back with open arms, as a *freed brother* in Christ. That is the Radical Paul in the letter to Philemon.

But a **Liberal**, and less tolerant, **Paul** writes in Colossians and Ephesians:

> *Slaves, obey your earthly masters in everything, not only while being watched and in order to please them, but wholeheartedly*, fearing the Lord. Whatever your task, put yourselves into it, as done for the Lord and not for your masters, since you know that from the Lord you will receive the inheritance as your reward; you serve the Lord Christ. For the wrongdoer will be paid back for whatever wrong has been done, and there is no partiality. *Masters, treat your slaves justly and fairly*, for you know

---

[A] Philemon 8–22

that you also have a Master in heaven.[A]

And a **Conservative Paul** appears in Timothy and Titus:

Let all who are under the yoke of slavery regard their masters as worthy of all honour, so that the name of God and the teaching may not be blasphemed. *Those who have believing masters must not be disrespectful to them on the ground that they are members of the church*; rather they must *serve them all the more*, since those who benefit by their service are believers and beloved.[B]

Tell slaves to be submissive to their masters and to give satisfaction in every respect; they are not to talk back, not to pilfer, but to show *complete and perfect fidelity*, so that in everything they may be an ornament to the doctrine of God our Saviour.[C]

No Gender Discrimination in Christ

Along the shoreline of ancient Ephesus there is a mountain called Bülbül Dag, and on the northern slope there is found a cave which has become a grotto with an image of the apostle Paul (we know it's Paul because his name is etched in Greek). There is a female saint beside him called Thecla with her mother-in-law Theocleia next to her. There has been discovered an apocryphal book called the *Acts of Thecla*, which was quite popular in the second century CE. It is a Christian romance of Paul's influence upon young Thecla while she was a virgin. Paul had converted Thecla after she heard him preach and was reflecting on a future life of chastity.

Both figures have their hands raised—which is an indication of teaching. Both are of the same stature—which, in ancient iconographics, is the sign of equality: stature equals status. However, the right hand of the image of Theocleia has been burnt and her eyes have been gouged out.

[A] Colossians 3:22–4:1; Ephesians 6:5–9
[B] 1 Timothy 6:1–2
[C] Titus 2:9–10

A Tale of Two Saviours

Christian Grotto on Mount Bülbül Dag, Ephesus

We imagine a time when men and women were thought to be of equal status, and that someone came later and destroyed that equality, because it violated the hierarchical structure of the typical Roman paterfamilias. Someone entered the grotto and defaced the icon and denied the woman her right to teach. Such denigration of women exists in the conservative and liberal presentations of Paul in the New Testament.

Cave Icon of Saint Paul, Thecla and her mother-in-law Theocleia

The **Radical Paul** wrote in Galatians:

There is no longer male and female, for all of you are one in Christ.

And the **Radical Paul** in Romans also recognised the status of women:

I commend to you our sister Phoebe, a deacon of the church at Cenchreae, so that you may welcome her in the Lord as is fitting for the saints, and help her in whatever she may require from you, for she has been a benefactor of many and of myself as well. Greet Prisca and Aquila, who work with me in Christ Jesus, and who risked their necks for my life, to whom not only I give thanks, but also all the churches of the Gentiles. Greet also the church in their house. Greet my beloved Epaenetus, who was the first convert in Asia for Christ. Greet Mary, who has worked very hard among you. Greet Andronicus and Junia, my relatives who were in prison with me; they are prominent among the apostles, and they were in Christ before I was.[A]

A **Liberal Paul** in Ephesians and Colossians commands that:

Wives, be subject to your husbands as you are to the Lord. For the husband is the head of the wife just as Christ is the head of the church, the body of which he is the Saviour. Just as the church is subject to Christ, so also wives ought to be, in everything, to their husbands. Husbands, love your wives, just as Christ loved the church and gave himself up for her.[B]

Wives, be subject to your husbands, as is fitting in the Lord. Husbands, love your wives and never treat them harshly.[C]

But a **Conservative Paul** in Timothy and Titus dictates:

I desire, then, that in every place the men should pray, lifting up holy hands without anger or argument; also that the *women should dress themselves modestly and decently* in suitable clothing, not with their hair braided, or with gold, pearls, or expensive clothes, but with good works,

---

[A] Romans 16:1–3, 7
[B] Ephesians 5:22–33, 6:5–9
[C] Colossians 3:18–25, 4:1–2

as is proper for women who profess reverence for God. *Let a woman learn in silence with full submission. I permit no woman to teach or to have authority over a man; she is to keep silent.* For Adam was formed first, then Eve; and Adam was not deceived, but the woman was deceived and became a transgressor. Yet she will be saved through childbearing, provided they continue in faith and love and holiness, with modesty.[A]

Tell the *older women* to be reverent in behaviour, not to be slanderers or slaves to drink; they are to teach what is good, so that they may encourage the young women to love their husbands, to love their children, to be self-controlled, chaste, good managers of the household, kind, *being submissive to their husbands*, so that the word of God may not be discredited.[B]

In Search of the Historical Paul

Summarising the inconsistencies in the teachings of Paul, as found in the Pauline letters, leads to a consideration of three possibilities:

1) that the injunctions in the pastoral letters, Ephesians and Colossians cannot be reconciled with the visionary ideals and practices outlined in Paul's authentic letters to the Galatians, Romans and Philemon
2) that Paul was not the author of the three pastoral letters, and that the letters to the Ephesians and Colossians, if by Paul, had been amended
3) that Paul altered his views as time went on before his death.

Addressing the possibilities in order, is it not reasonable to assume that if it was so necessary for someone to order such prescriptive behaviour as is found in the pastoral letters, it must be because it *was precisely what was going on in the Pauline churches,* that *Gentiles were accepted alongside Jews in Christian fellowships without the preconditions of circumcision and kosher,* that *women were teaching in the ecclesias,* and that *slaves were given their freedom in Christian households,* practices which were at odds with the hierarchical structure of the paterfamilias Roman household?

[A] 1 Timothy 2:8–15
[B] Titus 2:3–5

The credo expressed in the letter to the Galatians stands in contrast to the prescriptive injunctions of the pastoral letters; the contrary prerequisites cannot be reconciled. The task offered to Phoebe—which we may assume was typical of Paul—is discordant with what was written by the authors of the letters to the Ephesians and Colossians. Conservative and critical scholars, in general, agree that the pastoral letters of Timothy and Titus could not have been written by Paul, but were written at a later time by a Christian scribe who had attempted to *de-radicalise Paul*. Furthermore, the letters to the Ephesians and Colossians reflect a later setting and context (and theology) compared to those of Paul's earlier works. However, not every conservative scholar holds this view.

Regarding the pastoral letters of Timothy and Titus, the three documents again presuppose a more structured setting of the Christian Church than is reflected in the first letter to the Corinthians (and 1 Thessalonians): the literary styles, emphases and theological perspectives of all three pastoral letters are inconsistent with the teaching outlined in the authentic letters. There's too much stress on authenticity to render them beyond suspicion.

The letter to Philemon is exceptionally earnest: every sentence is charged with the Christian imperative to *have Onesimus back and grant him freedom in Christ*. Paul was aiming to *convert Philemon* in three literary ways:

1) by appealing to his better nature and sense of goodwill

2) by use of familiar terms of human attachment: 'my child', 'my heart', and 'if you consider me your partner, welcome him as you would welcome me,' and by offering to pay the debts of Onesimus

3) by reminding Philemon of the value of Onesimus to them both.

Paul earnestly pleads with Philemon to *have Onesimus back as a freed man: A Christian master cannot own a Christian slave within the household of faith.* When Paul corresponds with Rome he delivers a letter through a courier named Phoebe. He wants the congregations in Rome to accept her as an apostle and a teacher in the *ecclesias*; Phoebe would not be expected *to be silent and inferior in status to her male believers.* At the close of the Roman letter, Paul cites two female believers by name, Mary and Junia. Mary, he writes, worked 'very hard' and Junia (along with Andronicus), he writes, was 'prominent amongst the apostles'. What clearer evidence do we need to show that Christian women were of equal status to men in the *ecclesias*, that they taught and led in collective worship, since all are one in Christ? The pastoral letters don't reflect the practice of the Pauline churches, but the mind of *someone aiming to de-radicalise Paul and make him a conventional citizen* within Roman society.

The last question can be answered by means of a simple test. Paul wrote letters to the Romans and Philemon whilst under house arrest—they are authentic to Paul. One inference in the letter to the Romans (Paul's final testament) is that Christian men and women were of *equal status in Christ*. Given that the letter to the Romans was probably the last letter we know of, it is implausible to reason that he altered his outlook at the close of his life. If Paul was nothing else, he was consistent—as is evident in the letter to the Galatians regarding the issues of kosher and circumcision, where he opposed Cephas and James, and in the letter to the Corinthians, where he argued that circumcision was irrelevant for pagan converts.[A]

Footnote

We note a similar injunction in 1 Corinthians, an early letter of Paul:

> *If anyone speaks in a tongue*, let there be only two or at most three, and each in turn; and let one interpret... (As in all the churches of the saints, women should be silent in the churches. For they are not permitted to speak, but should be subordinate, as the law also says. If there is anything they desire to know, let them ask their husbands at home. For it is shameful for a woman to speak in church...). So, my friends, be eager to prophesy, and do not forbid *speaking in tongues*.[B]

However, the passage reflects the hand of the censor *de-radicalising Paul*. That it was an embellishment is evident by its different location in early manuscripts. When the injunction is read in the current context, the flow of argument of 'speaking in tongues' (*glossolalia*) is disrupted (verses 33b-

---

[A] Galatians 1:9–14, 5:2–6; 1 Corinthians 7:17–19
[B] 1 Corinthians 14:27–40 (33b–36)

36 are set in parentheses to show their positions in the manuscripts: some have the injunction following verse 33a, and others have it after verse 40). The interpolation also contradicts injunctions made early on in the same letter which assume *women were permitted to speak in church:*

> *Any woman* who prays or prophesies etc.; *brothers and sisters*, I do not want you to be uninformed... God has appointed in the church first *apostles*, second *prophets*, third *teachers*; then deeds of power, then gifts of healing, forms of assistance, *forms of leadership*, various kinds of tongues...[10]

Such embellishments in ancient manuscripts were not uncommon at the end of the first century, a practice not unique in documents of antiquity. As an aside, we note similar injunctions are found in two New Testament letters attributed to Peter, which can hardly be authentic (Chapter 8).[11]

Notes

[1] Borg and Crossan 2009.

[2] Crossan: YouTube Lecture: https://www.youtube.com/watch?v=ZJiPpAnFe4A.

[3] There were believers along the Italian coast at Putteoi (Acts 28:13-14) and we have evidence of Christians being at Pompeii: Wright 2018: 384.

[4] Crossan and Reed 2005.

[5] Paul could not win over pagans of the *boulé*, since they were obliged to offer animal sacrifices to the gods of the city: Crossan and Reed 2005.

[6] Crossan 2008: 1 Corinthians 15:34-35. I thank Ian McHaffie for pointing this out.

[7] Ehrman 2018.

[8] Wright 2018: 282.

[9] The ideal *vision* of Galatians 3:28-29 could not be required for those outside the household of faith. Paul knew slavery couldn't easily be abolished, as slaves and Roman masters were the social structure that held the Empire together. Paul's Radical *vision* applied only for those in the *ecclesias*, hence 1 Corinthians 7:21-24.

[10] 1 Corinthians 11:2-16, 12:2: Ehrman 2012: 243-245.

[11] 1 Peter 2: 18-21; 1 Peter 3:1-4.

4

Paul: A Light to the Nations

Introduction

With the close of the New Testament period, history knows of only three evangelists comparable with Paul. The successes of the Gospel mission to accept Jesus in the early decades was due to him and his decision to free the teaching of Christ from the Law — principally by removing the Jewish requirements of circumcision and kosher for salvation (Chapter 5). In this chapter we examine the journeys of Paul, the theme of his Radical Gospel of Christ crucified and risen, and what drove him onward in his quest to reach Spain. What was the Radical Gospel he taught that first opened the door to the Gentiles? And who actually was the historical Paul? We need first to recognise that the New Testament portrays four characteristics of Paul. We have Paul the Greek philosopher, Paul the missionary, Paul the theologian and Paul the apocalyptic prophet.

Paul: the Greek Philosopher

Paul stands on the Areopagus (renamed Mars Hill by Rome) to deliver a sermon to Epicurean and Stoic philosophers.[1] The message of the sermon was not characteristic of anything written in letters regarded as authentic to Paul, which begs the question of how much of Luke's portrayal of him in Acts is historical. The sermon was suited for a philosophical audience, where the apostle Paul gave a philosophical lecture on the nature of God, the Creator of heaven and earth, a God which cannot be represented with graven images. There is a footnote to the resurrection of Jesus, but apart from that the core of the sermon is not Pauline, and is more in tune with Lucan theology. The account by Luke in Acts concludes with the sequel that many Athenians scoffed at him and went away, some followed him, but others said they would hear him again. Are we listening to Paul here, or is the sermon the creation of Luke speaking through Paul (a common technique in ancient documents)? This is a question raised repeatedly in studies of Paul.

Study of St. Paul Preaching in Athens, Raphael, 1514–1515

I am not disputing whether the account on Mars Hill was historical. Paul was an educated and articulate Jew of the diaspora, but we don't read of him arguing in such a way in his letters as we find in Luke's report of his mission in Athens.[2] And furthermore, Luke's Greek is considered to be of the finest amongst the works of antiquity. Was Luke redacting a story for an educated readership? Given that historical accounts are seldom value-neutral, and that they all have agendas, we ask: how much of what Luke wrote about Paul generally is authentic? We are certain about one Lucan depiction, which is the itinerary of Paul's missionary expeditions.

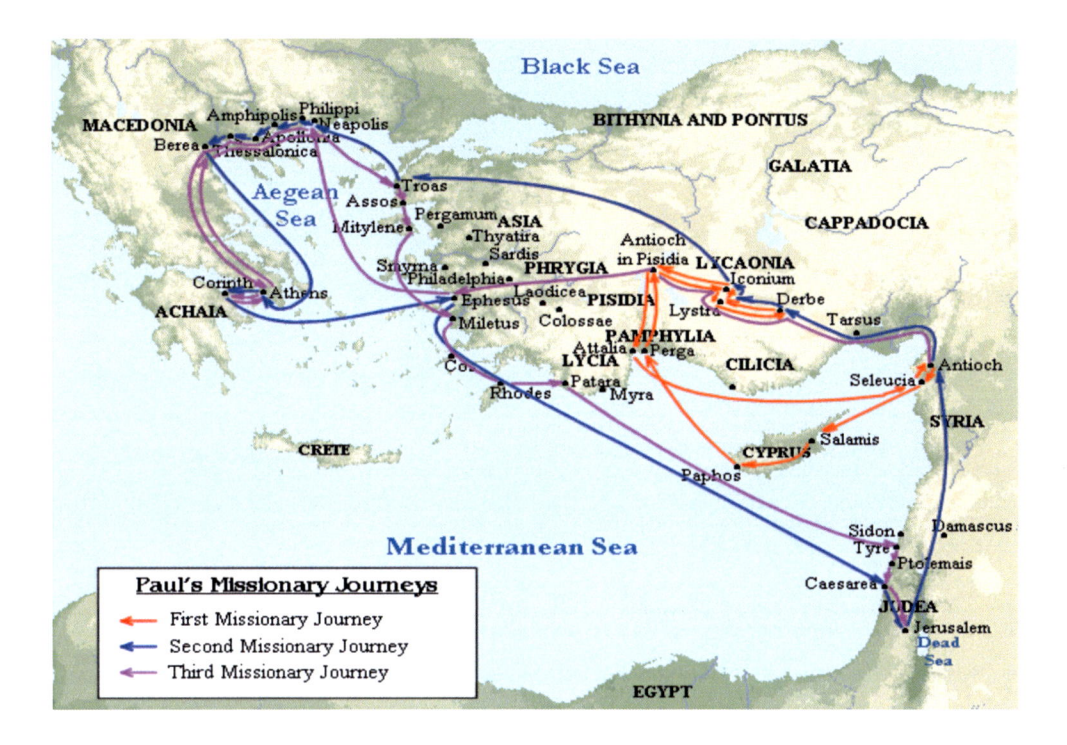

Paul: the Christian Missionary

The Jewish mission of the Jerusalem community to convert Jews was not nearly so effective as the Pauline mission to convert pagans. Had it not been for the expansion of the Gospel throughout the Mediterranean cities of the Greco-Roman world, it would have died out, as a further sect of Judaism, as took place for the Pharisees, the Sadducees, the Essenes and the Ebionites, and for the apocalyptic sectarians who wrote the Dead Sea Scrolls. Consider the map above and note the extent of Paul's journeying to convert pagans to Christianity ('pagans' and 'Gentiles' are terms used interchangeably to describe polytheistic people which are neither Jewish nor Christian).

According to Luke, Paul travelled on three occasions to Galatia (Turkey), twice to Asia and Macedonia, and once to Achaia (modern-day Greece), returning twice to Jerusalem before being escorted to Rome under armed guard. By any stretch of the imagination, this is an exhaustive itinerary for first-century conditions of travel. Paul and his evangelising comrades evidently had a determined sense of mission-consciousness, a conclusion drawn by most historians of Paul. Martin Goodman writes:

On the basis of a thorough examination of every significant piece of ancient pagan and Jewish evidence, the evangelising mission of the Christian church was unparalleled and unprecedented.[3]

McMullen writes 'After Saint Paul, the church had no mission.'[4]

Another scholar estimates that, from an itinerary prescribed in Acts, Paul would have travelled more than 10,000 miles.[5] His *modus operandi* wasn't to stay any longer than necessary in any one town or city, but to establish a community and leave. Paul's letter to the Romans was probably written in Corinth. In that letter he says there was no longer 'any room for work in these regions'.[A] Paul's longer-term aim when reaching Rome was to go on to Spain, where, according to the worldview, he would have reached the 'end of the world', so that the 'full number of the Gentiles' (he hoped) had received Christ, and 'all Israel [he hoped] would be saved'.[B] He went from synagogue to synagogue, from city to city, until he was rejected by fellow Jews, or imprisoned by the authorities. In the letter to the Romans he said he had taken the Gospel 'from Jerusalem to Illyricum' (though we have no source material of any preaching in Jerusalem or Illyricum).[C] He laboured to support himself as a leatherworker to avoid being dependent upon the charity of others.[D]

The author of Acts might have misplaced the first missionary journey of Paul. In Luke's scheme, the first missionary journey through Asia Minor served as the backdrop for the Apostolic Council in Jerusalem, in support of the speeches given by Peter and James, and to announce the decree; to show how the first mission of Paul and Barnabas was authorised by the apostles. Luke knows nothing about Paul's early mission in Arabia, Syria or Cilicia that Paul recounts in such precise dates and places in the letter to the Galatians. Bornkamm considers it inconceivable that Barnabas and Paul would not have gone to Cyprus, the native country of Barnabas, or the neighbouring districts of Southern Asia Minor, which had such large Jewish populations.[6]

[A] Romans 15:23
[B] Acts 13:47; Romans 10:13–15, 11:25–26
[C] Romans 15:19
[D] Acts 18:3; 1 Corinthians 4:12

Paul: the Theologian

The Jewish Gospel

Acts has authentic source material of (largely, Peter's) preaching subject matter of early Jewish Christianity. It contained six principal features:

   a) Jesus performed many signs and miracles.
   b) He was crucified but God raised him, as predicted in Scripture.
   c) God confirmed Jesus as the Messiah (King) by his resurrection.
   d) Israel rejected Jesus.
   e) Jesus has been exalted to heaven, as predicted by the prophets.
   f) Having faith in Jesus, repenting converts could receive the Spirit.[A]

This corresponds fairly closely to the Gospel of Paul outlined below. The two issues of dispute in the early Jesus movement, which caused a major division in Jewish-Gentile Christianity are minimised in Acts (Chapter 5).

The Gentile Gospel

The previous narrative in Acts to the incident at Athens covered the story of Paul preaching at Thessalonica. Two principal features of his theology appear in the narrative:

   a) Jesus was the Messiah spoken about in Scripture.
   b) The Jewish Messiah had to suffer before rising from the dead.

The theology of Paul's Gospel, as articulated in the authentic letters, can be summarised as propounding five principal teachings:

   a) Jesus was the Jewish Messiah, as pre-ordained in Scripture.
   b) Jesus was crucified at the will of the Jewish leaders.
   c) God raised Jesus on the third day, as recorded in Scripture.
   d) Jesus was exalted to heaven, and would return to judge the world.
   e) By faith in Jesus, pagans can escape *wrath* and enter the Kingdom.[B]

If we ask by what means salvation came, Paul was quite explicit:

> We preach Christ as crucified.[A]

[A] Acts 2: 14–36, 3:11–26, 4:8–31
[B] 1 Thessalonians 1:9–10, 13, 4:14–18; Galatians 1:1–3; Romans 1:1–4, 15, 3:23–24; 1 Corinthians 1:17, 23–24, 2:2; Philippians 2:7–11, 18–21, 3:10–11

The crucified and resurrected Christ was central to Paul's proclamation, and since his main conversions were pagans, he needed to demonstrate how they could become right with God (made to be righteous), which he achieved in his theology of justification by faith:

> Those who are *righteous by faith* shall live.[B]

> But now is God's *righteousness* apart from law revealed…

> God's *righteousness through faith in Jesus Christ for all who believe*. For there is no distinction: all have sinned and fallen short of God's glory and *are justified* without merit by his grace, through the *redemption in Jesus Christ*…[C]

Convicted Messiah

Gentile Christians have to have faith in Jesus as *Lord* for salvation. These teachings can be found in every authentic letter of Paul. How he became aware of a crucified Messiah is unclear—our earliest sources are silent on the matter—but, as said above, the early Jewish Christians in Jerusalem may have worked out the link between an executed Jew and the Messiah before Paul. He, as did most Jews of the day, conceived of the militaristic Son of David, and he, as did many Palestinian rabbis of the time, knew of the Deuteronomistic curse on anyone hung from a tree (i.e. crucified):

> When someone is convicted of a crime punishable by death and is executed, and you hang him on a tree, his corpse must not remain all night upon the tree; you shall bury him that same day, for *anyone hung on a tree is under God's curse*.[D]

Notice how Paul turns the contradiction in terms to become the solution to an Israelite mystery:

> Christ *redeemed us* from the curse of the law by *becoming a curse* for us—for it is written, 'Cursed is everyone who hangs on a tree'—in order

---

[A] 1 Corinthians 1:23
[B] Romans 1:16–17
[C] Romans 3:21–30; Galatians 2:15–16, 3:6–9
[D] Deuteronomy 21:21–23

that in Christ Jesus the blessing of Abraham might come to the Gentiles, so that we might receive the promise of the Spirit through faith.[A]

Paul's logic is strained. The Jews, he reasons, put their reliance upon the Torah (the Law), but the Torah prescribes that anyone failing to honour its prescriptions is *cursed*: Jewish purists, therefore, cannot be saved:

> For it is written, 'Cursed is everyone who does not observe and obey all the things written in the book of the law.'[B]

Paul calls on his Galatian audience to consider why they had received the Holy Spirit (as a seal of divine approval) when not Jewish through birth. They acknowledge (in silence) that they have the Holy Spirit. Paul draws upon the Genesis narrative where God promises Abraham's progeny (i.e. every naturally-born Jew) an eternal inheritance of land and a perpetual race of descendants. But the last promise to Abraham featured a forecast beyond the orbit of Judaism, that *all nations* were to be blessed through Abraham. The Scripture (foresaw that God would justify the Gentiles by faith) declared the Gospel *beforehand* to Abraham:

> 'All the Gentiles shall be blessed in you.' For this reason, those who believe are blessed with Abraham who believed.[C]

Paul's thesis is that Abraham was acknowledged as a righteous man, not because he was circumcised, or because he was Jewish (Abraham was an Aramean), but because he *believed* in God.[D] In other words he had faith, which is precisely what Paul had claimed was at the heart of the Radical Gospel. By having faith in the Lord Jesus *you* (Gentiles) were to be saved. But if Jews rejected Jesus as their Messiah, and put their sole trust in the Torah that renders them 'cursed', they have no means of salvation. Christ became a curse (under the Law) to redeem Jew and pagan from the curse of failure to observe the Torah. It was an extremely hard sell: it failed to

---

[A] Galatians 3:13
[B] Galatians 3:10 / Deuteronomy 27:26
[C] Galatians 3:8–9 / Genesis 12:1–3
[D] Deuteronomy 26:5

convince the Jews, but the Gentile 'God-fearers' who attended the Jewish synagogues of the diaspora were drawn to Paul's Gospel.

Because Christians are so familiar with the details of the crucifixion and resurrection of Jesus, it is often underestimated how radical this teaching would be for a Jewish, let alone a Gentile audience. Every known Jewish writing and apocalyptic material leading up to this period pointed to the model of the military monarch fighting on behalf of the Jewish nation to liberate the people from oppressive domination by foreign powers.[7]

The concept of a Jew, of all people, executed as a criminal of Rome, being the future Caesar to rule over a worldwide Empire, the Kingdom of God, would be counter-intuitive and counter-cultural, but it was central to the Radical Gospel Paul delivered to the pagan world. Paul promoted a rival Sovereign and *Saviour* of the world, which was going to be more superior than Emperor Augustus, Tiberius, Caligula, Claudius or Nero could ever have been. Luke's Paul has close connections with the Jesus movement in Damascus, and the Jerusalem church; he represents Peter as instrumental in launching the Gospel of Christ crucified and raised, but, in the letter to the Galatians, Paul implies this wasn't the case. Paul had become isolated from the Jerusalem church; he attributed his calling to convert the pagans to his personal *revelation of Jesus Christ*.

Paul was evidently a spirit enthusiast, but pressing for precise definitions of his accounts has not proved fruitful. How he personally became aware of Jesus being the Messiah is a mystery; it may have been a combination of pronouncements by the early believers he was persecuting (admiring their conviction and persuasion) and his contemplation of doubt over his resolve to destroy them during reflective moments (along the Damascus road, or the period in the Arabian desert where he withdrew for a while).

Paul: A Light to the Nations

We observed in Chapter 3 the very different pictures of Paul presented in his own testimonies compared with the recollections of him by Luke in Acts and the Deutero-Pauline documents, but a further contradiction in Christian sources is over who first opened the door to the Gentiles.

Paul: A Light to the Nations

The Gentile mission for Luke was a collective task, starting with Peter in Jerusalem forecasting from Joel that *all flesh* (nations) were to receive the Spirit and hear the Gospel preached in their *native language*. The mission of Stephen follows (a *Hellenistic* convert, i.e. a Gentile), followed by Philip preaching the Gospel in Egypt and baptising the *Ethiopian* eunuch. Simon Peter required a vision and a heavenly instruction to overcome his racial objection before baptising Cornelius, a *pagan centurion* of Caesarea. Paul's position, within Luke's scheme, was in being a member of the missionary outreach of Jerusalem in spreading the Gospel to the ends of the earth. But how did Paul view his role in the divine scheme?

Paul never conceived of himself converting from Judaism to Christianity, but as becoming a true Israelite, seeing the risen Christ as the fulfilment in Judaism of what God had revealed in Jewish Scripture. Could he have considered himself to be the one predicted by Isaiah to be God's Servant in bringing 'Light to the nations', a prophecy Matthew applied to Jesus?[8]

> I am the Lord, I have called you in righteousness, I have taken you by the hand and kept you; I have given you as a covenant to the people, a light to the nations... [wrote Isaiah].

> I will give you as a light to the nations, that my salvation may reach to the end of the earth... [predicted Isaiah].

> I heard the voice of the Lord saying, 'Whom shall I send, and who will go for us?' And I said, 'Here am I; send me!' [wrote Isaiah].[A]

> I will confess you among the Gentiles [recalled Paul in Romans].[B]

> And I said, 'Who are you, Lord?' And the Lord said, 'I am Jesus whom you are persecuting. But rise and stand upon your feet, for I have appeared to you for this purpose, to appoint you as a servant and witness to the things in which you have seen me and to those in which I will appear to you, delivering you from your people and from the Gentiles—to whom I am sending you to open their eyes, so that they may turn from darkness to light and from the power of Satan to God, that they may receive

---

[A] Isaiah 42:6–8, 49:1, 6
[B] Romans 15:9–12; Galatians 1:15–16; 2 Corinthians 4:4–6

forgiveness of sins and a place among those who are sanctified by faith in me.' [reported Luke of Paul in Acts].[A]

This missionary objective didn't apply to the historical Jesus: Jesus said he was 'sent to the *lost sheep of Israel*'.[B] Paul was fully aware of the special significance of the Jews in God's eyes. After all, as he said in the letter to the Romans, to the Jews came the promises from which the Gentiles were to benefit. He hoped and trusted the Jews would accept Christ in the end (i.e. before it was too late), as he predicted: 'All Israel will be saved...'.[C]

Paul in his strident Galatian testimony not only declares an *exclusive* role in opening the door to the Gentiles, but also adds that Cephas, James and John, and the collective Jerusalem church, agreed that this was the case:

> But when God, who had set me apart before I was born and called me through his grace, was pleased to reveal his Son to me, so that I might proclaim him among the Gentiles, I did not confer with any human being, nor did I go up to Jerusalem to those who were already apostles before me, but I went away at once into Arabia, and afterwards I returned to Damascus...
>
> Those who were supposed to be acknowledged leaders... contributed nothing to me. On the contrary, when they saw that I had been entrusted with the gospel for the uncircumcised, just as Peter had been entrusted with the gospel for the circumcised (for he who worked through Peter making him an apostle to the circumcised also worked through me in sending me to the Gentiles), and when James and Cephas and John, who were acknowledged pillars, recognised the grace that had been given to me, they gave to Barnabas and me the right hand of fellowship, agreeing that we should go to the Gentiles and they to the circumcised.[D]

Furthermore, Paul writes in Romans that he had fulfilled the Scripture by taking the Gospel to the Gentiles; he quotes Isaiah to endorse his mission

---

[A] Acts 26:15–18
[B] Matthew 10:6, 15:24
[C] Romans 9:1–5, 27–29, 11:26
[D] Galatians 1:16–17, 2:6–10

to reach 'the ends of the earth'.[9] Ehrman writes: 'Paul's calling to preach was anticipated in the Jewish Scriptures.'[10]

Paul: An Apocalyptic Prophet

Paul changed his allegiance from persecutor to apostle for Christ, but he remained a Jewish apocalyptic and was convinced, like Jesus before him, that the end of the age was about to arrive. Paul's apocalyptic message was most descriptively portrayed in the first letter to the Thessalonians, where Paul spoke of an impending *wrath* before the return of Christ.

> The people of those regions report about us what kind of welcome we had among you, and how you turned to God from idols, to serve a living and true God, and to wait for his Son from heaven, whom he raised from the dead—Jesus, who *rescues us from the wrath that is coming.*[A]

Ehrman's summary is apt: 'The comment is terse but illuminating.'[11] Paul has other apocalyptic forecasts of the *Parousia*:

> We declare to you by the word of the Lord, that we who are alive, who are left until the coming of the Lord, will by no means precede those who have died. For the Lord himself, with a cry of command, with the archangel's call and with the sound of God's trumpet, will descend from heaven, and the dead in Christ will rise first. Then we who are alive, who are left, will be caught up in the clouds together with them to meet the Lord in the air; and so we will be with the Lord forever.

> Listen, I will tell you a mystery! We will not all die, but we will all be changed, in a moment, in the twinkling of an eye, at the last trumpet. For the trumpet will sound, and the dead will be raised imperishable, and we will be changed...

> Why do you pass judgment on your brother or sister? Or you, why do you despise your brother or sister? For we will all stand before the judgment seat of God. For it is written: 'As I live, says the Lord, every knee shall bow to me, and every tongue shall give praise to God.' So then, each of us will be accountable to God.

[A] 1 Thessalonians 1:9–10

At the name of Jesus every knee should bend, in heaven and on earth and under the earth, and every tongue should confess that Jesus Christ is Lord, to the glory of God the Father.[A]

Winning Souls for Christ

Paul was a devoutly religious Jew in respect of the Torah. He records two confessions of devotion regarding his past life under Judaism:

Circumcised on the eighth day, a member of the people of Israel, of the tribe of Benjamin, a Hebrew born of Hebrews; as to the law, a Pharisee; as to zeal, a persecutor of the church; *as to righteousness under the law, blameless.*

Are they Hebrews? So am I. Are they Israelites? So am I. Are they descendants of Abraham? So am I. Are they ministers of Christ? I am talking like a madman—*I am a better one: with far greater labours...*[B]

With Christ having been *revealed to him*, all that pent-up passion for the cause of Judaism was re-channelled in renewed endeavour to convert the Gentiles to the living God (from the dead gods of paganism), to avoid the *wrath* of God and to wait for the Day of Salvation. From his apocalyptic worldview, we see what spurred him onward to get to Spain, and given his expectation of the imminent *Parousia*, it is not difficult to understand his sense of urgency.

Summary

Paul doesn't appear to have had a successful mission in Athens. Since we know of no Pauline *ecclesia* in Athens in this period, Luke's portrayal of the sequel is probably historical. In spite of losing a battle at Athens with two schools of philosophy, Paul had won the war on the universal scale. Constantine opened the political door for Christian faith to flourish, but Paul had opened the cultural door for the pagans to come through. How he did this will be examined in the next chapter.

[A] 1 Thessalonians 4:15–17; 1 Corinthians 15:51–52; Romans 14:10–14 / Isaiah 49:6; Philippians 2:10
[B] Philippians 3: 5–6 / 2 Corinthians 11:22–23

We have as much chance of studying the psychology of Paul as we have of the historical Jesus. Even though we have better sources (the writing of Paul compared with no known writing by Jesus), they are inaccessible for such an exercise (against Tom Wright). The missionary commitment and drive of Paul comes through, however, when he becomes emotive about an important issue. In such cases (as in Galatians), we see his passionate indignation over anything which stood in the way of preaching Christ to the Gentiles. The extent of his journeys illustrates his endeavour to take the Gospel to the 'ends of the earth', but how he viewed his role in the divine plan to save pagans from the *wrath* of God remains conjecture.

Notes

[1] Epicureans believe the gods are indifferent to humans. Stoics argue that the divine spark is everywhere present in the universe, like a fire or spirit that animates the whole universe and that will eventually blaze out in a great moment of conflagration, and then repeat itself in never-ending cycles (Paul was a near contemporary of Seneca [4-65 CE], a famous Stoic philosopher).

[2] The speech of Paul from the Parthenon (temple) at the Areopagus (governing council) on the Acropolis was not a philosophical debate, argues Wright, but a trial where Paul was charged and heard. I cannot see the evidence for this. Paul walks free with no charges brought against him—this was not Luke's intention. Socrates was charged in Athens at the same location for corrupting the youth and introducing foreign divinities: Wright 2018: 196.

[3] Ehrman 2018: 117.

[4] Ehrman 2018: 118.

[5] Ehrman 2018: 58.

[6] Bornkamm 1971: 43-44.

[7] 'When Rabbi Akiba declared in AD 132 that Simeon ben Kasiba was God's Messiah, this meant that Simeon was now the ruler of a small Judean State in rebellion against Rome.' Wright 2018: 105. The Bar Kokhba revolt marked the end of a long line of Jewish revolts, and in 132-135 marked the end of the Jewish State: summarized in Lines 2017.

[8] Ehrman 2018: 58-73.

9   This prophetic fulfilment was denied by Matthew (the most Jewish of all the evangelists), who applies the prophecy to Jesus, a particular trait in Matthew, which doesn't occur in Mark, a Pauline Gospel, on which he was dependent:

> Now when Jesus heard that John had been arrested, he withdrew to Galilee. He left Nazareth and made his home in Capernaum by the sea, in the territory of Zebulun and Naphtali, so that what had been spoken through the prophet Isaiah might be fulfilled: 'Land of Zebulun, land of Naphtali, on the road by the sea, across the Jordan, Galilee of the Gentiles—the people who sat in darkness have seen a great light, and for those who sat in the region and shadow of death light has dawned.' From that time Jesus began to proclaim, 'Repent, for the kingdom of heaven has come near.' (Matthew 4:12-17 / Isaiah 9:1).

Other possible contending Scriptures include the prediction of the messenger at the death of King Uzziah, which Mark applies to Jesus: Isaiah 6:1-13/2 Kings 15:1-7 / 2 Chronicles 27:2.

10 Ehrman 2018: 56.

11 Ehrman 2018: 65.

5

The Gentile Controversy

The Conversion of St Paul, Palma El Joven, 1544

A Jewish male would daily recite:

Thank you God for not making me a Gentile, a woman or a slave.[A]

Introduction

Scholars have recognised for some time the contradictions between Acts and Paul's letter to the Galatians over the Gentile mission. Although we have considerable documentary evidence of Christian activity in the late first to the early second century, not much is known from the 30s to the 50s, apart from pre-source material in the Gospels and passing references

---

[A] Jewish-authorised Babylonian Talmud: *Menahoth* 43b–44a

to the early Jesus movement in the book of Acts. We may speculate, but we have nothing substantial to go on.[1]

Luke informs the 'most excellent Theophilus' of his painstaking attention to genuine source material, but the record of the Jesus movement in Acts is biased and selective. Luke presents the early community of Jerusalem as being *unified* and *harmonious* in teaching and practice, but this was not the case: the accounts in Acts are selective and idealistic. In claiming that the early followers of Jesus were in *complete agreement* and of *one accord* contradicts details in Paul's letter to the Galatians. Before studying these contradictions in detail, we must examine the religio-ethnic context of the Gentile controversy.

The Setting of the Jerusalem Assembly

The twelve apostles and first followers of Jesus from Lower Galilee were poor and unschooled, what we might classify as *rural peasants*.[2] When the Gospel reached a wider Roman audience of the elite and more educated classes, the nature of the community changed. Paul was an educated Jew, a Pharisaic teacher, and a zealous follower of the Torah, who was able to construct an argument and engage in discourse on Hebrew Scripture.

No Gospels (as they exist today) were in circulation when Paul wrote to the early churches, and there were no documents about Jesus (Sayings or deeds), but only oral traditions and fragmentary sources. Moreover, Paul had never met Jesus, and only had brief meetings with Simon Peter, first in Jerusalem and later at Antioch.

Paul is emphatic about not receiving his Gospel from the twelve apostles; the three 'Sayings of the Lord' he cites were probably recalled from oral tradition.[3] He was familiar with details of Jesus' last week, but appears to have no interest in biographical facts about him as a Jewish prophet—he views Jesus as a trans-historical figure.

Luke's book of Acts did not exist when Paul wrote to the Galatians. The major controversy during the first two decades wasn't about the Gentiles entering the Jesus movement, but about what they were expected to do after conversion. Paul's account in the letter to the Galatians is *the only first-hand source* we have available. The letter to the Galatians represents Paul's (unchallenged) position, and serves as evidence of only one side of a two-sided dispute; we have no counter-claims by James, Cephas (Peter) or the Judean party of believers.[4]

Luke's account ought to be read as a retrospective account of events that happened 30 to 40 years earlier than when it was compiled: *it isn't what a historian regards as a primary source*. The letter to the Galatians was written five years after the dispute: *it is a primary source*. These are the significant dates of the controversy:

- the death of Jesus: 30–33 CE
- Paul's conversion: *c.* 34, shortly after the crucifixion
- the Jerusalem assembly: 47–52
- the letter to the Galatians: 50–55
- Luke's record in Acts: 85–95, some 35–40 years after Galatians.

The ministry of Jesus was directed exclusively to Palestinian Jews, but a few Jewish Christians had a greater vision. As the Gospel spread abroad, these Jewish converts experienced opposition and rejection by their own fellows but reception by Gentiles aligned to Judaism at the synagogues in the cities and towns of Asia Minor (Galatia: Turkey). Christian numbers increased rapidly during the first decades as Gentile converts entered the fellowships, but this created racial problems. Tensions were mounting in mixed assemblies of Jewish and Gentile Jesus followers eating together in defiance of the kosher regulations.

The tangible marker of identity for Jewish males—a son of Abraham and member of the covenant people—had always been circumcision, and the Jews viewed themselves as God's chosen nation (a belief shared by Paul). Circumcision was a rite of passage for all Jewish men, but Greco-Romans honoured masculinity and abhorred physical mutilation: Roman athletes performed nakedly in Roman theatres and Olympic games. According to Jewish custom, it was *anathema for circumcised Jews to eat or to worship with uncircumcised* Gentiles: it was culturally offensive. So how could the Jesus community celebrate together the Lord's Supper?

This was the dilemma. If Christianity was not to become an obsolete sect within Judaism, the problem of kosher had to be resolved. As Jesus said nothing (that is known) about circumcision, and a failure to compromise would end with segregation, one side had to give way. The drama was played out at two centres (Jerusalem and Antioch), and between five key players: Peter, James and John, Paul and Barnabas.

The Principal Issue of Discord

The Jesus movement was facing a new situation: *should Jewish and Gentile believers worship in separation, or congregate together in one united assembly? Must Gentiles be circumcised to be in fellowship?* This was the purpose of the meeting. However, the records are divergent. One source depicts the rite of circumcision and table fellowship as the main issues, and the other has meat given to idols and sexual depravity as points of discord. According to Acts, *the church at Antioch appointed* undisclosed believers to join Paul and Barnabas to go to Jerusalem to settle the issue after Judean followers instructed pagan converts they had to get circumcised for salvation, but, for Paul, he and Barnabas initiated the meeting *after a revelation*.

Luke presents the meeting as a Council; but Paul describes it as a private meeting. Luke claims the Council reached an *amicable agreement*; but Paul implies the dispute remained *contentious*. Luke presents group relations as cordial, where all parties were unanimous in agreement; but Paul saw them as fractious. Cephas behaved liberally at Antioch when abroad, but prejudicially when Jewish delegates arrived from Jerusalem. The records are also divergent regarding:

- the dating and sequence of events
- the solutions arrived at
- the roles played by leading protagonists.

The Gentile Controversy

There are contradictions between Paul's testimonies (Pauline letters) and Luke's presentation of him (Acts) in respect of his early life as a Pharisaic Jew, and his activity in Jerusalem, principally:

- Paul's education and activity in Judaism
- Paul's conversion and persecution of early Christians
- the number of visits of Paul to Jerusalem before the meeting
- the role of Paul (against Peter) opening the door to the Gentiles
- the prescriptions imposed upon Gentile converts
- the relations between Paul, Barnabas and the Jerusalemites: Peter, James (the Lord's brother) and John, the son of Zebedee.

The Apostle Paul, Rembrandt, 1635

Paul's Schooling in Jerusalem

Luke narrates an occasion when an attempt was made on Paul's life by a Jewish mob following an accusation that he had defiled the Temple.[5] The Temple guards quelled the riot, and the Roman tribune arrested him. In defence, Luke's Paul relates the events of his former life in Judaism:

> I am a Jew, born in Tarsus of Cilicia, but brought up in this city at the feet of Gamaliel, educated strictly according to our ancestral law, being zealous for God...[A]

'Gamaliel the Elder' (the grandson of Hillel the Elder) was the principal authority of the Sanhedrin Council in the mid-first century. In Christian tradition, he was known as a distinguished Pharisee and an expert on the Jewish Law. Luke viewed him as sympathetic to the Jesus movement. He is mentioned again in Acts, as exercising prudent judgement when Peter was arrested and dragged before the Sanhedrin: his advice was to release Peter and cease opposing the Christians, since they were not identified as potential messianic charlatans (such as Theudas and Judas of Galilee had been). Luke reports him as saying:

> If this plan or this undertaking is of human origin, it will fail; but if it is of God, you will not be able to overthrow them—in that case you may even be found fighting against God![B]

Scholars have questioned the authenticity of this report on the basis that such a distinguished Jew would hardly support a radical Jewish sect that might prove a threat to Judaism.

We have *a first-hand account* of Paul's early life in Judaism in the letter to the Philippians, but Gamaliel is not mentioned, which is surprising, since it would have supported his argument to do so. Paul had been:

> Circumcised on the eighth day, a member of the people of Israel, of the tribe of Benjamin, a Hebrew born of Hebrews; as to the law, a Pharisee; as

---

[A] Acts 22:3
[B] Acts 5:38–39

to zeal, a persecutor of the church; as to righteousness under the law, blameless.[A]

The Conversion on the Way to Damascus, Caravaggio, 1601

Paul's Damascus Conversion

Luke presents three versions of Saul's conversion on the Damascus road: the first relates the event, and the other two are embedded in speeches of Paul to a Jewish, and a Gentile (Roman) audience.[B] The accounts have a

---

[A] Philippians 3:5–6
[B] Acts 9:1–19, 22:3–16, 26:9–18

few contradictions and have been coloured by Old Testament epiphanies and legendary calls to mission. They are inconsistent with the account of Paul in the letter to the Galatians.[A] Luke introduces Paul by his Semitic name Saul, as one of the witnesses to the stoning of Stephen, a diaspora Jewish convert, and the first Christian martyr. Saul was instrumental in persecuting the early believers in Jerusalem. He had been commissioned by the high priest with letters of authority to apprehend Jewish converts at Damascus and bring them bound to Jerusalem.

Luke is unaware of any early missions of Paul in Arabia over the 16-to-17 years period, twice the period it took to complete his letters. Bornkamm thinks this is significant.[6] It is wrongly assumed that the region of Arabia was unoccupied desert. There were large cities of non-Jewish inhabitants in the east of what we now refer to as Jordan: there was Petra where Paul suffered persecution from Aretas IV (9 BCE–40 CE), the Nabatean ruler.[B] Paul had no success in Arabia, which might explain his visit to Cephas in Jerusalem.[C]

Regarding the epiphany of Jesus in Acts, Paul is completely silent. It was clearly a life-changing experience, but he only talks of it in a general way. Bornkamm (along with other critics) thinks the epiphany was a fictitious creation by Luke, as it's consistent with Luke's scheme of Acts. There are contradictions in what was seen and heard, and the commission by Jesus. Bornkamm writes: 'Acts makes his missionary work in the Gentile world originate at Jerusalem.'[7] Luke reduces Paul to a prominent representative of the Apostolic Church. Luke's Paul was not an *apostle* outright (as Paul thought of himself), since Luke's Jesus only appointed twelve apostles.[D]

For Bornkamm, his conversion was a cognitive re-conceptualisation:

> Through arguments with the Hellenistic Christians in Damascus and elsewhere, whom he had originally hated and persecuted, it suddenly dawned on him whom this Jesus really was whom hitherto he

---

[A] Galatians 1:16–24
[B] 2 Corinthians 11:32; Acts 9:23
[C] Galatians 1:17
[D] Luke 6:12–16; Acts 1:13, 26

regarded as the destroyer of the most sacred foundations of Jewish faith and whom it had been right to crucify.[8]

We are not to assume Saul converted from **penitent sinner to saint**: quite the contrary, as he boasted. He was a devout Jew who was compliant in observing the Torah. Saul's conversion was in *attitude and direction* not in conduct and fervency. He converted from zealous Jew to zealous apostle of Christ, in regarding the Jewish rite of circumcision and the importance of the Torah as refuse compared to knowing Christ Jesus.

The Assembly in Jerusalem

The Record of Luke in Acts

The first appearance of Paul in Acts is as a Pharisee from Jerusalem who was party to the martyrdom of Stephen (*c.* 35 CE). Luke claims that Saul approved of Stephen's martyrdom, and that Paul 'ravaged the Church by entering house after house', dragging off men and women to prison. The narrative breaks to cover the mission of Philip in Samaria.[A]

The first account of Paul's conversion on the Damascus road is preceded by a report of him 'breathing threats and murder against the disciples of the Lord'. The high priests of Jerusalem had prepared letters for Paul to deliver to the synagogues at Damascus authorising him to arrest men or women belonging to what Luke describes as 'the Way'.[B]

Following his conversion, Saul of Tarsus (first mention of Tarsus) met up with Ananias in Damascus, who welcomed him with reluctance into the community. Luke writes of Saul preaching 'Christ as the Son of God and Messiah' to the Jews in the synagogues, and that the disciples helped him escape through a hole in the wall because some Jews had plotted to kill him. So, Saul lived in Jerusalem (*inferred*) before travelling to Damascus. There follow *four return visits* to Jerusalem:

1) Saul returns to Jerusalem from Damascus (*his first return visit*) to escape from the Jews. He preached boldly and was accepted by the Jerusalem

---

[A] Acts 8:1–13, 26–40
[B] Acts 9:1–30

church, but had to escape to Caesarea, and on to Tarsus and further persecution (this time from the Hellenists).[9]

2) A description follows of a (*second return*) visit to Jerusalem by Saul and Barnabas to bring food and relief for the believers in Judea because of a famine.

3) There follows a legendary narrative of King Herod's death and another (*the third return*) visit to Jerusalem by Saul and Barnabas, along with John Mark.[10]

4) Paul and Barnabas are summoned to Jerusalem (*the fourth return*) to settle the dispute over (uncircumcised) Gentile converts.[A]

According to Luke, the meeting was prompted because:

> Certain individuals came down from Judea to Antioch and were teaching the brothers, 'Unless you are circumcised according to the custom of Moses, you cannot be saved.'[B]

Luke states that Paul and Barnabas had *no small dissension and debate with them*, and that believers *in Antioch had recommended the visit to Jerusalem* to discuss the issue with the 'apostles and the elders'. He reports they were *well accepted* after relating their missionary successes in Asia. The trouble began when Pharisaic believers insisted that converts *had to be circumcised* in accordance with the *Law of Moses*. Peter delivers a speech against this view from his experience of the conversion of Cornelius and his receiving of the Holy Spirit, which is supported by Paul and Barnabas from their successes. The meeting is formally closed by James (leader of the church at Jerusalem) with the proviso that Gentile converts, whilst free from the Jewish rite of circumcision and observance of the Torah, *must nevertheless abstain from sacrificial meat* and *sexual immorality* and *meat which has been not fully bled* (kosher):

> We should write to them to abstain only from things polluted by idols and from fornication and from whatever has been strangled and from blood.[A]

[A] Acts 15:1–35
[B] Acts 15:1

The Gentile Controversy

The Jerusalem Council *agreed unanimously* and wrote in confirmation. A decree was dispatched with two prominent believers to accompany Paul and Barnabas to authorise the joint decision of the Council.

The Record of Paul in Galatians

The letter to the Galatians (*c.* 53 CE) was Paul's apologia to the cluster of *ecclesias* he established in Galatia. It was an appeal for believers to accept his position against that of Jewish-Christian propaganda and opposition; it serves as his defence over an important issue that arose in Antioch. In anguish, Paul pleads:

> I am astonished that you are so quickly deserting the one who has called you [i.e. me] in the grace of Christ and are turning to a *different gospel*.[B]

Paul condemns the (undisclosed) 'false believers spreading confusion' by preaching a 'different gospel'. *The opposition must be of Christian and Jewish persuasion*, therefore, be *Jewish Christian* i.e. converted Pharisees.[11]

Paul presents a defence, as though standing on trial in a court of law. He writes that the Gospel he preached hadn't come from human beings but from a *revelation of Jesus Christ*. Paul summarises his early life in Judaism, of which they were presumably well aware, how he:

- 'violently persecuted the church of God and tried to destroy it'
- was 'well advanced in Judaism' amongst his peers
- was 'zealous for the traditions of my ancestors'.

Paul recounted his early life in Judaism before *God revealed his Son to him to proclaim Jesus amongst the Gentiles*. There follows a record of the 'private meeting' called in Jerusalem to settle the dispute over Gentiles entering the fellowship. Paul's recollection of the meeting follows this sequence:

1) After the revelation, he spoke with no one, but went away at once into Arabia, and then 'returned to Damascus' (details not covered in Acts). He insists he didn't speak with any of the apostles.

[A] Acts 15:20, 29
[B] Galatians 1:6

2) After 'three years' he 'went to Jerusalem to visit Cephas', lodged for 'fifteen days', met 'James, the Lord's brother', and went into the regions of Syria and Cilicia. He says he was unknown amongst the churches of Judea, but he acknowledged they would have known of his reputation. He insists again that he was telling the truth: 'Before God, I do not lie!'

3) After fourteen more years (seventeen years after conversion, 51 CE, three or four years before the date of the letter), he went to Jerusalem again with Barnabas and Titus. He doesn't say he was sent for, or that he was appointed, but that he was called through a *revelation*. He talks of his mission to the Gentiles 'in a private meeting with the *acknowledged leaders*', and he also claims his Greek convert Titus did not have to undergo circumcision. He stresses that he did not submit to 'false believers', 'slipped in to spy out the freedom we have in Christ Jesus'.

Paul denounces the *acknowledged leaders* who 'contributed nothing to me'. He asserts he was commissioned with the Gospel for the Gentile mission, and that the assembly ratified his commission:

> They saw that I had been entrusted with the gospel for the uncircumcised, just as Peter had been entrusted with the gospel for the circumcised.

Paul confirms that James, Cephas and John (the *acknowledged pillars*) were in complete agreement that this was God's plan. To seal the decision they (Paul and Barnabas) were granted the 'right hand of fellowship', with the request that the prosperous Greco-Roman believers (Gentiles) should be mindful of their poor brethren in Judea. Peter, according to Luke, denied the claim in a speech given at the Council. Luke's Peter reported:

> My brothers, you know that in the early days God made a choice among you, that *I should be the one through whom the Gentiles would hear the message of the good news and become believers.*[A]

But the polemic doesn't end here. Paul reports that when Cephas visited Antioch his conduct was hypocritical. Paul scolds Cephas because when 'Certain people came from James' to Antioch Cephas refused to eat along

---

[A] Acts 15:7 (10, 11:3)

with the uncircumcised Gentile converts, whereas prior to their arrival he had no problem eating together. So, previously, the Jewish Christian and Hellenistic Christian believers—circumcised and uncircumcised—shared the same table in fellowship. Besides this hypocrisy by Cephas, Barnabas, Paul's companion in the mission, was 'led away by their hypocrisy' also.

Paul scolds Cephas publicly:

> If you, though a Jew, live like a Gentile [*when James and his delegates are not present*] and not like a Jew, how can you compel the Gentiles to live like Jews [*just because the Jerusalem party are here*]?

Paul concluded by emphasising the freedom that every Jesus follower— Jew and Gentile alike—has through faith in the Lord Jesus, and that faith in Jesus was in contrast to justification through the works of the Law, by which he meant circumcision in adherence to a covenant God made with Abraham for every Jewish male. This testimony varies considerably from Luke's account in Acts.

Historicity of the Gentile Controversy
Paul of Tarsus in Jerusalem

The first confusion to clear up is over the pre-Christian activities of Saul. Was the Lucan detail of Saul's period in Jerusalem an accurate account? Luke presented Paul residing in Jerusalem and being taught by Gamaliel, whilst acknowledging that his home had been in Tarsus. Nowhere in the authentic letters of Paul is this said or implied. We know Saul persecuted the Jesus community initially, but was it at Jerusalem (as said by Luke), or at Damascus and/or Antioch (as said by Paul)? We don't know, but in light of Luke's theological interest in Jerusalem as the centre from which the Gospel spread abroad, and given that Paul's account in the letter to the Galatians is so specific, and that he is presented in the Council in Acts as just a passive spectator instead of a principal protagonist, we question Luke's account of Paul's education and persecution in Jerusalem.

There is a further historical inaccuracy in Acts. The Jewish priests weren't permitted under Roman jurisdiction to arrest and bind Jewish 'offenders' and march them to Jerusalem for punishment. The Jews weren't allowed to execute their own justice, apart from 'beating fellow Jews with rods' in the synagogues for religious offences of blasphemy. Jewish officials were required to get consent from the administration for capital punishment.[A] Furthermore, the Judean political system had no official jurisdiction over the Roman province of Syria through the first century. The notion of Saul at Damascus dragging unwilling Jesus believers to Jerusalem is fanciful.

The Issue of Circumcision for Paul

We also question whether Luke's account of Paul agreeing to circumcise Timothy (of Greek and Jewish descent) at Lystra is historical, since Paul in Galatians argues persuasively that Titus (also of Greek descent) 'was not forced to be circumcised' when entering Jerusalem. That Paul should take an uncircumcised convert to meet up with the apostles in Jerusalem is intriguing. Was Paul making a point? Was it an ultimatum? It appears a provocative act in a delicate situation. He obviously had no intention of circumcising Titus to satisfy the orthodox Jewish followers of Jerusalem.[B]

The orthodox Jewish followers of the Jerusalem party arriving at Antioch may not have been emissaries appointed by the apostles. We take note of the Jewish descriptions in the letter to the Galatians. There were:

- *certain individuals*
- *false believers* secretly brought in… to spy on the freedom…
- **apostles** *before me*, and
- ***supposed acknowledged leaders*** [who] contributed nothing to me.[C]

The first two groups must represent a different category of believers than the latter two—they being the apostles—but, even so, not a little derision is voiced towards the *acknowledged leaders* in the letter to the Galatians (against Bornkamm).

[A] Acts 9:1–2
[B] Galatians 2:5
[C] Galatians 2:1–14

Secondly, if the apostles had agreed that the mission of Paul was for the *uncircumcised*, just as the mission of Cephas was for the *circumcised*, what was the point, and therefore the basis, of Luke representing Simon Peter as requiring a heavenly vision to receive Cornelius (Roman Gentile) into the fellowship, a narrative that Dibelius regards as a literary invention of the author, and as having no historical basis?[12]

The Jerusalem Assembly

The events leading up to the meeting in Jerusalem of Paul and Barnabas with Peter, James and John over the Gentile controversy has brought to the fore the difference between the writing of history and theology.

The Jesus community attracted Greco-Roman converts more wealthy and literate than many Jews of Lower Galilee, and missionary experience had shown—through the effort of farsighted followers, such as Paul—that the expanse of early Christianity in converting Greeks was at the expense of the Jews turning their backs on the Gospel and denying the crucified and risen Messiah. But this resulted in cultural tension. How were people of different backgrounds to integrate within a common fellowship?

Contradictions in Acts and Galatians

The accounts of Acts and Galatians have contradictions that illustrate the different perceptions of how serious the issue of the Gentile admission to the people of God had been. Luke *minimised* the conflict in Antioch, but Paul viewed it as *controversial and fractious,* where heated disagreements led to fallouts amongst the chief parties. Which account is dependable?[13]

The Case Against Luke's Account

We don't know whether Luke had access to Paul's letter to the Galatians when he wrote Acts. He represents the meeting as a formal Council with speeches delivered by Peter, Paul and Barnabas to 'all the apostles and the whole assembly', and a summing up by James, the most conservative member of the meeting. The official correspondence to authorise the joint decision and decree was a conventional conclusion in historical literature of the period; it was important to Luke, as it is cited again at Lyconia, but it is curiously unknown to Paul.[A]

Paul argued against two obligations of the decree (abstention from food offered to idols and kosher) in the two letters Corinthians and Romans, which suggests that Luke (or a source) made up the Decree. Was Luke—writing 35 to 40 years later—*harmonising contentious events to represent the Jesus movement as more united than it was in fact*? Luke's Gospel presented Jesus as a Jewish prophet through and through: he had been circumcised on the eighth day, according to the Jewish custom. The evangelists were all in favour of the Gentile mission. Luke has the Gospel going out from Jerusalem to Samaria, Antioch, Syria and Ethiopia and on to Rome. Luke has Peter being the first apostle to bring the Gentiles into fellowship, but was it historical? Was Luke's theological and literary interest overriding accurate history?

Luke presents the Jerusalem Council as an outworking of the Holy Spirit; Paul presents it as a dichotomy of two missions—him to the Gentiles and Peter to the Jews (Luke's Peter is positively disposed towards the Gentile mission through the narrative of the conversion of Cornelius).

The Case Against Paul's Account

We have good grounds to reason that since Paul's letter was a *first-hand source* composed close to the period to which it makes reference, it ought to be considered the most accurate version of events. But, then, Paul had his own agenda, his own axe to grind. His standing and authority had not been strong, since the tradition had clearly shown that:

- Peter was the *first disciple and the leader of the Jerusalem church*
- Peter had *first-hand experience of the mind of Jesus*
- Peter *sat at the feet of Jesus*, and had direct knowledge of the mind of Jesus in delivering the good news of the Kingdom *exclusively to the Jewish people*.

[A] Acts 15:19–20, 28–29, 16:4

How could Paul contest the opinion of the apostle Peter? Then there's the (silent) apostle John. Added to which, there's James, the brother of Jesus in the flesh. If Luke's record of the mother and siblings of Jesus coming around to accept the Gospel of the crucified and risen Jesus is historical, the views of James cannot be dismissed. *Could Paul claim greater authority than that of being the Lord's brother?*

This is a persuasive argument, given that the norm amongst Jews during the times of Jesus was of dynastic bloodline descent: the priesthood and the aristocracy, the Pharisees and bandits adopted hereditary succession. Kingship was crucial in a messianic movement based upon a legitimacy of Davidic descent. Should not the same argument apply to the 'mother church' of Jerusalem (after James died, the leader of the Jerusalem church was Simeon son of Cleopas, the cousin of Jesus)? Paul's Radical Gospel to the Gentiles had to take on a mountain of hereditary power.

The frustration voiced in Paul's letter to the Galatians (stronger in Greek than in English) implies that he had to be defensive; he even fell out with his companion Barnabas. Had his Radical Gospel truly reflected the good news of Jesus? In light of the ministry of Jesus being restricted to the Jews in the region of Galilee and Judea (not even Samaria), and targeted to the Palestinian Jews in place of those of the diaspora, we could say that *Paul had preached a different gospel*, that he distorted the Gospel of the historical Jesus. We might also think that he *protests too much* to make his position credible. His authority came not from Jesus' teaching disseminated from oral tradition, but from the personal *revelation of Jesus*. And one could say that that sounds all too subjective. After all, what does it mean?

We don't know what Paul discussed with Cephas when first they met. It is certain that Peter never resisted Paul from continuing to preach in the way he had done, that the meeting was cordial and that a Gospel without Torah and kosher was sanctioned by Cephas, otherwise Paul would have justified his stand, as he did at Antioch over the issue of table fellowship. It is also probable that they didn't wholeheartedly agree with each other, since it wouldn't account for why Paul was so insistent on being isolated from the Jerusalem community, and render the argument in the letter to the Galatians unintelligible. Perhaps they obligingly agreed to differ with each other and weren't able to foresee the social implications of a shared fellowship. It is certain that Cephas, the first disciple to be called, and the initial leader of the Jerusalem church *never corrected Paul and put him right*: 'A crash course in missionary work with Peter can be ruled out', pressed Bornkamm.[14] Perhaps, as Dibelius argues, we should distinguish between historical truth and literary-theological truth in Christian Scripture:

> We must have only one account of the meeting between Paul and those in authority in Jerusalem, that of Paul in Galatians 2... Paul refers to a revelation, Luke to a decision made by the community, but both can ultimately be reconciled. Luke's treatment of the event is only literary-theological and can make no claim to historical worth. The final result, the Apostolic Decree, did not originate in this meeting.[15]

Luke appears to have few details of the early assembly in Jerusalem apart from a gathering of the apostles with Paul to discuss the issue of Gentile admission to the Jesus movement. He knows of a decree in circulation, as it is mentioned twice (first announced by James, and secondly put on the lips of Paul), but the setting of the Apostolic Decree is likely to have been formulated at a later time than the period of Paul. The existence of such a decree, agreed by Paul, at this assembly renders the statement 'those [the *acknowledged*] *leaders* [apostles] contributed nothing to me' unintelligible. Luke's theological purpose was to demonstrate how an election to admit the Gentiles into the Christian community had been authorised by God: a) by his application of Peter's vision, and the subsequent conversion and granting of the Holy Spirit to Cornelius; b) through the mission of Paul in Galatia; and c) by proxy of the Jerusalem church through a declaration of James: 'For it has seemed good to the Holy Spirit...'.[A]

Chronology of Events

How can we reconcile the contradictions in the two sequences of events? Paul claims he went to Jerusalem *only once* before the assembly, but Luke records him returning to Jerusalem *on three occasions* before the Council, this meeting being the *fourth visit*. Historical data and dates are known to

---

[A] Acts 15:28

be questionable in the book of Acts—they are considered untrustworthy. The precise outline of Paul's itinerary (in years and locations) in a context of independence from the Jerusalem apostles does read as authentic.

Barnabas

Finally, we have the separating of Paul from Barnabas. Was their fallout due to the kosher-circumcision controversy alone, where Barnabas aligns himself with Cephas in refusing to dine alongside Hellenistic Christians, or was it Paul's reluctance to take John Mark on a new missionary tour?

Paul was frustrated about John Mark pulling away midway through the first mission, and didn't want to risk taking him again, according to Acts. Their disagreement was said by Luke to be 'sharp', but later in Acts Luke says that Paul and Barnabas *parted amicably*. In the letter to the Galatians, Paul states the conflict was *substantial*, and was based not on a decision to take John Mark on a further mission but on an insistence that the Gentile converts should have to be circumcised to take part with Jewish believers in the Lord's Supper: even Barnabas was 'led astray by their hypocrisy' (i.e. in going along with the orthodox Jewish Christians in not sharing the same table as Gentile converts).

For Peter and Barnabas, it may have been a pragmatic decision when in the company of more conservative Jewish believers, but for Paul *the unity of Christian fellowship was at stake* (dining and worshipping together being cultural symbols of Jewish acceptance). We do not know how the Gentile controversy ended, but it seems that from this time on he was no longer associated with the Antioch community, and that he became *persona non grata* in the Jerusalem church. His operational centre could have been at Ephesus or at Corinth, we are not sure, but it certainly wasn't at Antioch.

Concluding Summary

A schism occurred between the Jerusalem and Pauline churches, initially led by James, Peter and Barnabas on one side, and Paul and Silas on the other.[16] By isolating the early traditions from Acts, we see how it was that two Hellenised Jewish converts, Stephen and Philip, broke away from an all too Jewish-centred Jesus movement. The evangelists were of different branches of the Church and shaped their Gospels accordingly.[17]

There's a tendency for the casual reader to select the accounts of Acts in preference to those in Paul's letter to the Galatians in cases where there's confusion, because Acts does read as a chronological history—the author claims he checked his source material.[A] Perhaps Paul overstated his case in Galatians? But the personal testimony in the letter to the Galatians was a first-hand account by the author (it is the *primary source*), whereas Luke compiled Acts decades later, when the controversy over the Torah being applicable to Gentile converts to Christianity became a distant memory. When Luke composed Acts in the late 80s, the Jewish Temple, the centre of Judaism, had fallen and the circumcision issue had been resolved.

As history turned out, Paul had saved the Gentile mission from isolation and being ostracised from an all too Jewish-centred Jesus religion. Luke presented the Church as led by the Holy Spirit, and the Christian Gospel spreading out from Jerusalem to Rome under persecution, but with no internal threat. Did Luke manufacture Paul's early time in Jerusalem and Judea, and his dependence upon the apostles (*the acknowledged leaders*), to minimise the conflict that occurred at Antioch in the early 50s?[18]

Notes

[1] The church at Antioch was founded by unknown missionaries of Cyprus and Cyrene, arising from persecution after the death of Stephen: Acts 11:19–26:

> Now those who were scattered because of the persecution that took place over Stephen travelled as far as Phoenicia, Cyprus, and Antioch, and they spoke the word to no one except Jews. But among them were *some men* of Cyprus and Cyrene who, on coming to Antioch, spoke to the Hellenists also, proclaiming the Lord Jesus…

The text also covers the appearance of Barnabas and the Hellenists (Greeks) in relation to the foundations of the Church. We have no idea of who founded the churches in Rome or how it was founded.

[A] Luke 1:1–4

2   The terms 'disciples' and 'apostles' for Christians are used synonymously by some authors of the books of the New Testament, but the author of Acts, in the early chapters, describes the twelve disciples of Jesus as the 'apostles' to distinguish them from other 'disciples' (Acts 6:1-2), or 'believers', or 'saints in Jerusalem', particularly in summaries. Luke often addresses them by name (Peter, Philip, Stephen etc.), but when he comes to the conversion of Saul, he describes the followers at Damascus as 'disciples' (a wider following, as distinct from the apostles). It is amongst this broader community led by Ananias of the church at Damascus that Saul receives tuition of the new faith (Acts 9:10-22).

3   Students and biblical critics have been surprised that Paul rarely quotes a Saying of Jesus. There are two exceptions to this, both are found in the letter to the Corinthians. Paul affirms the teaching of Jesus on the inseparable nature of marriage and the prohibition of divorce (1 Cor. 7:10), and the right of the Christian missionary to receive provision as a gift when preaching the gospel (1 Cor. 9:14). The former is derived from Mark 10:2–12, and parallels, and the latter from Q. (Matthew 10:10/Luke 10:7). Sometimes Paul says that he thinks he has a command of the Lord when exercising his judgement on a matter. Paul was, however, conversant with the crucifixion and the resurrection of Jesus, and with the institution of the Last Supper; and there are examples of Paul's ethical teaching which are a rephrasing of, or are reminiscent of, the ethical teaching of Jesus. Paul knows at least one parable of Jesus: 'The Thief in the Night' (1 Thess. 5:2/Luke 12:39–40). There are instances where Paul's teaching varies with the teaching of Matthew's Jesus: compare Romans 10:13 with Matthew 7:21.

4   According to John 1:42, Simon Peter, the son of Jonas (John), was renamed Cephas, which is Aramaic for 'stone' or 'rock'.

5   Paul's arrest in Jerusalem in 57 CE occurred during a chaotic time in Judea. A year earlier, the *Sicarii* slaughtered the high priest Jonathan and began their reign of terror, murdering some of the priestly aristocracy. Messianic fervour was boiling over. Theudas was slain in 44 CE for messianic aspirations, and the rebellious sons of Judas the Galilean, Jacob and Simon, were crucified in 46 CE. The bandit chief Eleazar, the son of Dinaeus, who slaughtered Samaritans in the name of God, was beheaded by Felix, the Roman procurator, and 'the Egyptian' who appeared on the Mount of Olives in 57 CE, professing he would bring the walls of Jerusalem down, had escaped (his followers were rounded up and were slaughtered). For James and the apostles in Jerusalem this period could have

meant the end of the age and the return of Jesus. His job was to sort out Paul when he appeared in Jerusalem in 57, a probability which Luke seemed keen to obscure: Aslan 2014: 194.

6   Bornkamm 1971: 26-30.

7   Bornkamm 1971: 24-25.

8   Bornkamm 1971: 23.

9   Acts 9:23-29. There is another break in the narrative where Luke records the preaching activities of Peter and his heavenly vision to preach Christ to the first Gentile, Cornelius. Luke claims Cornelius converted and was baptised. There was criticism from the Jerusalem brethren, until Peter convinced them that this was the will of God made evident through the Holy Spirit. We then read how the message spread abroad because of persecution after the stoning of Stephen. There is detail of Barnabas being sent to Antioch from Jerusalem, and of Saul being brought from Tarsus to Antioch.

10 They are received by the Jerusalem community and experience a call of the Spirit to take the message out to the Gentiles, or the 'God–fearing' Hellenists (Greeks), as the author describes them. Luke's understanding of this radical decision was that it was because the Jews stirred up trouble and persecuted Saul (now addressed by his Greek name Paul), whilst the Gentiles had been receptive to the Gospel. Paul and Barnabas returned to Antioch to share the news of the Gentiles becoming Christians in Asia Minor.

11 Some might argue that the opposition consisted of Jews, and that they were not Jewish Christians, but this is unlikely. Codex Bezae (the *Western text*) refers to 'Christian Pharisees' in place of '*certain individuals* came down from Judea', and that they were 'teaching the brothers'. They had to have been Christians to be given access to the church to preach. Furthermore, at the Council, although they are described as 'false believers', they also belonged to the 'sect of the Pharisees', as indeed Paul had once been a Pharisee. And, again, given that he speaks of them preaching 'a different gospel' and 'spreading confusion', they must have been converted Jews (Jewish Christians). The *Western text* also has a sharper presentation of the conflict.

12 For students wishing to study the Jerusalem Council/assembly issue further from a literary and theological perspective beyond history, I recommend Charles Williams (1975: 177–185) for a scrutiny of the different renderings in the two manuscripts, Michael Goulder (2009: 1–7) for an accessible, though controversial,

discussion of the issues, and Martin Dibelius (1956: 93–101) for a full critical analysis of the book of Acts. Dibelius links the release of Peter from prison in Jerusalem with the subsequent release of Paul and Silas from prison in Philippi. The narrative of Peter's escape (Acts 12:5–17) is clearly an untarnished legend which was current amongst Christians, he writes, and which Luke utilised. Whereas, in the release of Paul and Silas from prison at Philippi, the citing of the earthquake is secondary to the point of the story, which Dibelius regards as a Lucan creation. The author has used the story to illustrate how Gentile converts were brought into the community; it was a genuine Christian tradition (Dibelius 1956: 20–24).

[13] Wright (2018: 163f.) thinks that Paul didn't refer to the 'Jerusalem conference' described in Acts 15, so we cannot be sure what he thought about it. He says that Paul makes much of the unity arising from the event. I have examined his argument, and it appears a weak apologetic; it is as though his reasoning is directed by a predisposition towards the records not being fallible. Paul is most emphatic in the letter to the Galatians about refusing to circumcise Titus before the Jerusalem assembly, but, latter in Acts, Luke has Paul circumcising Timothy. Wright avoids the inconsistency by applying the principle in 1 Corinthians 9:20-22: when preaching to the Jews, I become Jewish; when preaching to the non-Jews, I become non-Jewish. In preaching the Gospel, this might be a reasonable principle: namely, that Paul will argue from the Torah to convert a Jew and from philosophy to convert a Greek. The argument cannot apply to Paul at the assembly, where his whole raison d'être was to stand his ground; that the Gospel cannot be constrained by the imposition of Jewish rites of circumcision foisted upon the Gentiles: it applied to the old covenant of the Jews.

Moreover, Paul relates his calling to go to Jerusalem as a 'revelation', so as to make the point that he was not ordered by others to meet the Jerusalem Christians. For some bewildering reason, Wright applies the 'revelation' of Jesus to Paul to the incident outlined by Luke in Acts of the vision of Agabus (Acts 11:27-29) before a first missionary journey by Paul and Barnabas, which prompts Galatians 2:1-10. (Agabus crops up again in Acts 21:10-12 before Paul's final trip to Rome, a decade later in the autumn of 57.). However, the 'revelation' in Galatians clearly related to the visit to Jerusalem in 47/48, not to any wide-scale famine. Going along with Wright's sequence, the reference to the collection for the poor cited in Romans 15:25-26 and Galatians 2:9-10 doesn't make sense: Wright 2018: 95, 142-147, 75-176, 349-351, 383.

14 Bornkamm 1971: 28.

15 Dibelius 1956: 100.

16 Eusebius claims that Simeon and Hegesippus succeeded James as the leader of the Jerusalem church: Eusebius, *Ecclesiastical History* 3:11-12.

17 This is best illustrated in the way each evangelist represents the disciples of Jesus: Mark was a Pauline Christian, Luke a liberal Pauline, Matthew an anti-Pauline/pro-Petrine and John as an anti-Petrine. The embryonic community was split into two factions in the early first century.

18 Dibelius 1956. These questions remain unanswered:

   1) Was Paul a resident of Jerusalem and a persecutor of Christians in and around Jerusalem, or did the persecution take place in Syria?

   2) Were the decisions of addressing circumcision for Gentile Christians made in a private meeting, or a Council involving all the elders of the Jerusalem church?

   3) Did everyone agree that Gentiles should avoid eating anything that had been sacrificed to an idol, or was that an issue that continued to plague the churches for decades?

   4) Were the three requirements even discussed at this meeting?

   5) Was there an edict passed by the assembly to which Gentile converts should strictly adhere?

   6) Was the narrative of Peter converting Cornelius historical or was it a myth created to preserve a balance in status between Peter and Paul opening the door to the Gentiles? Dibelius writes:

   > We can see that the narrative of Cornelius is the work of the writer Luke. (Dibelius 1956: 95, 93-101)

6

From Jewish Prophet to God

The Pantheon (Greek: 'temple of all the gods') was built on a former temple

Introduction

We explore here the significance of the Radical Gospel of Paul to see how a crucified and risen Jewish Messiah related to Roman imperial theology. How was the message of a *divinised Jewish prophet* from Galilee *received* by pagans of the Roman Empire? There is substantial evidence of Christian missionaries converting considerable numbers of Greco-Roman citizens. Perhaps the familial sense of community and the moral codes of Judaism drew some reflective people from the depraved culture of Rome. Perhaps the restrictive codes of kosher diet and circumcision were social obstacles which Paul's teachings had addressed, but was there something else that attracted pagans to reject the deities and festivities of their forefathers for the exclusive God of the Christians?

If the Empire had been founded on conquest and military power, was the success of the Christian mission due to Paul's Messiah being believed to be a more powerful deity than any pagan deity of the pantheon?

The Pantheon was completed by Emperor Hadrian and dedicated around 126 CE

Ehrman believes that if Christians had not come to believe that Jesus was God, Christianity would have remained an obsolete sect within Judaism and become extinct. The divinity of Jesus Christ became the central topic after the New Testament period: from the late first to the fourth century with the formation of the Nicene Creed. How did early Christians form the idea, then, that Jesus was divine: that Jesus Christ came to be God?

We begin with a brief look at the Greco-Roman and Jewish mythological beliefs about human beings becoming divine, to see how conceptions of a transpersonal Christ in heaven may have been received by educated and illiterate pagans. Finally we briefly examine the first-century conceptual worldview *of power and miracle* in relation to modern understanding.

Greco-Roman Men Becoming Divine

Paul's Radical Gospel to the pagan 'God-fearers' had significant religious power. In the patriarchal culture of first-century Rome there were three ways in which a human being might become divine:

1. If generals were courageous or victorious on the battlefield, the gods would receive them into the heavenly realm to become gods.
2. If a male deity impregnated a human woman, their offspring would be half-divine and half-human.
3. If a deity descended from heaven to become a human being.

1. Romulus ascends to heaven and becomes deified

Romulus was the founder of the Senate and the city of Rome. According to Livy and Plutarch, a she-wolf suckled Romulus and his brother Remus when babes. Romulus turned out to be a heroic king, but one day a storm broke out during a military parade and he curiously vanished from view. Witnesses claimed they saw him rise to heaven, and myths began to form over his early life: one has Mars (his father) impregnating Rhea Silvia in a sacred grove. Romulus was generally believed to have become Quirinus, the god of *War*, the third most powerful deity of Rome.

Altar to Mars (the father of Romulus and Remus) and Venus

2. Hercules was born half-divine and half-human

The Roman playwright Plautus gives an account of the birth of Hercules. Amphitryon, the general of Thebes, was married to Alcmene. But Jupiter (Greek: Zeus) was lured by her beauty and came down to earth disguised as her husband, Amphitryon. Jupiter slept with her throughout the night and had sex with her till the early hours. Alcmene gave birth to two boys. Amphitryon naturally thought that he had made Alcmene pregnant, that both Hercules and Iphicles were his sons, but Hercules was born through Jupiter, born a demigod, whilst Iphicles was mortal, born of Amphitryon. As a demigod, Hercules became a human god, a *human-divine* being, who was endowed with strength and might: he wrestled with death, and once descended into the underworld.

Hercules and the Hydra

3. When Gods became human

The Roman poet Ovid (43 BCE—17 CE, an elder contemporary of Jesus) wrote *Metamorphoses*, a book about transformations in ancient mythology of deities taking on human form to interact with mortal men and women.

The observant reader may already have noticed the precedents in Roman mythology of Paul's Radical Gospel of the risen Christ, Luke's exaltation theology, and John's Logos theology of the Word living amongst humans as the Son of God. Literary images of the New Testament mirror many of the old myths of Romulus and Hercules, and the current myths of Julius Caesar and Caesar Augustus becoming divinised heroes, but it is seldom appreciated that precedents had already existed in Judaism and Hebrew Scripture. It is erroneously assumed that early Judaism was monotheistic, but the term 'monotheism' (belief that only one God exists), did not come into fashion until the sixteenth century of the modern era.

How Men Became Gods in the Jewish World

The Jews were not unfamiliar with beliefs about human beings becoming divine. They are found in the Hebrew Scriptures and Jewish traditions.

1. Men becoming divine: Enoch, Moses and Elijah

According to Genesis, Enoch 'walked with God' and ascended to heaven, the death of Moses is shrouded in mystery (*Assumption of Moses*, cited in Jude), and the prophet Elijah ascended to heaven in a whirlwind.

> Enoch walked with God after the birth of Methuselah three hundred years, and had other sons and daughters. Thus all the days of Enoch were three hundred sixty-five years. Enoch walked with God; then he was no more, because God took him.[A]

> When the archangel Michael contended with the devil and disputed about the body of Moses, he did not dare to bring a condemnation of slander against him, but said, 'The Lord rebuke you!'[B]

[A] Genesis 5:22–24
[B] Jude 1:9

> A chariot of fire and horses of fire separated the two of them, and Elijah ascended in a whirlwind into heaven.[A]

Moses and Elijah appeared in a transcendental epiphany on the Mount of Transfiguration; we assume they both had been men who became divine when they died. As the traditions are reflected in the Gospels, it is clear that they were prevalent throughout the first century.[1]

2. Gods impregnating women to produce demigods

In Jewish folklore, the Sons of God came down to earth and impregnated beautiful women:

> The Nephilim were on the earth in those days—and also afterward—when the sons of God went in to the daughters of humans, who bore children to them. These were the heroes that were of old.[B]

3. God becoming human

Hebrew Scripture once described the King of Israel as God (*elohim*).

> I address my verses to the king... Your throne, O God (*elohim*), endures forever and ever... Therefore God (*elohim*), your God (*elohim*), has anointed you with the oil of gladness beyond your companions.[2]

What would the first Christians think about Jesus of Nazareth ascending to heaven to sit with God? *If they were Jews*, the ascension resembles the divinations of Enoch, Moses and Elijah. *If they were Romans*, the ascension of Jesus is reminiscent of the divinations of Romulus, Julius Caesar and Caesar Augustus, the most powerful deities of Roman imperial theology?

How the Historical Jesus Became Divine

In answering the question of how Jesus came to be considered divine, we trace the development of Christian beliefs from early Christian sources to

---

[A] 2 Kings 2:11
[B] Genesis 6:4; Jude 6

the Nicene Creed. We search for indicators in the New Testament which led to the formulation of the Creed, the relationship of Jesus of Nazareth to the God of Israel.

New Testament Projections of Jesus

We have access to what early Christians believed in the 30s to the late 50s in the pre-Pauline formulae of Christ, the first letter to the Thessalonians, the earliest sources of Mark (where Mark and John agree independently), the Q Source (sources common to Luke and Matthew which aren't found in Mark), and the early sources in Acts (where Luke conceptualises from primitive tradition how Christians had thought about Jesus in the 80s).

Jewish Christians in Palestine first gave the title 'Son of Man' for Jesus, a tradition drawn from Daniel 7. A transition occurred from what God had done through Jesus of Nazareth to what He would do in the future: from past to future Christology. The 'Son of Man' title had a brief life. The next phase occurs through reflection on the implications of Jesus' resurrection. It is inconceivable that diaspora Jews would have referred to Jesus as the God of Israel during the first century, considering the exclusive nature of Judaism and the fear of blasphemy. Paul knew that Jesus had once been a human being:

> From now on, therefore, we regard no one from a human point of view; even though we *once knew Christ from a human point of view*, we know him no longer in that way.[A]

For Jesus to refer to himself as God would be blasphemous and counter-cultural, and for Jesus' family, the twelve disciples and Jewish peasants of Galilee to consider him remotely divine during the ministry would be implausible and profane: no Jewish man in the early first century would dare take on the name of 'God'. And we can find no textual precedent for Jesus claiming his own divinity in the earliest strata of Gospel tradition. Paul's first letter to the Thessalonians appeared in 49–50 CE, two decades after the crucifixion, and in that letter there is no indication of Jesus being

---

[A] 2 Corinthians 5:16; Galatians 3:16 / Deuteronomy 21:18–21 considered divine until the ascension.[A] The Gospel of Mark appeared in the late 60s. An early source in Mark shows that Jesus never considered himself as God. It is an authentic story of a rich man who asks Jesus what he had to do for eternal life. The reply was incidental to the import of the question, but it illustrates what first-century Jews had believed about the chasm that exists between humanity and divinity: Jesus said:

> Why do you call me good? *No one is good but God alone.*[B]

We have evidence of Greek-speaking Jewish and pagan Christians of the diaspora referring to Jesus Christ as divine towards the close of the first century. Luke reapplied the early sources of sermons attributed to Peter and Paul in Acts, which have a sense of primitive construction. Consider how Luke paraphrases a speech attributed to Peter:

> This Jesus God raised up, and of that all of us are witnesses. Being therefore exalted at the right hand of God, and having received from the Father the promise of the Holy Spirit, he has poured out this that you both see and hear… Therefore let the entire house of Israel know with certainty that God has made him both Lord and Messiah, this Jesus whom you crucified.'[C]

In the letter to the Romans, Paul speaks of:

> The gospel concerning his Son, who was descended from David according to the flesh and *was* declared to be Son of God with power according to the spirit of holiness by resurrection from the dead, Jesus Christ…[D]

A pre-Pauline hymn—'Jesus Christ is Lord'—cited by Paul in the letter to the Philippians might originally have been in Aramaic form and be from the early 40s CE.[E] Such formulae reflect what theologians call Exaltation Christology: through his death and resurrection, Jesus was given a name

---

[A] 2 Thessalonians 2:15
[B] Mark 10:18
[C] Acts 2:36, 13:32–33
[D] Romans 1:1–3
[E] Philippians 2:6–11

above every other name. Christian converts regarded Jesus as the Lord (*Kyrios*) of the Church, and Jesus is portrayed this way in the Gospels.[3]

Mark's Presentation of Jesus

In studying Mark, a picture of Jesus appears that gives us an insight into what early Christians were thinking and teaching about Jesus in the 60s. The theology of Mark's Gospel can be summed up by an ignorance of the family, the disciples and Jewish leaders over Jesus' identity. Throughout the storyline of Mark, everyone was trying to figure out who Jesus was, everyone except the demons. The author and readership know that Jesus is the Messiah and the Son of God because it is declared in the first verse.

Mark 2 covers the Jewish teachers who believed that Jesus exorcised the demons through Beelzebul, the prince of demons. Mark 3 has the family of Jesus attempting to pull him away for being 'out of his mind'. In Mark 4 (the Seed collection of parables), the disciples and the Galileans have no idea what Jesus is talking about. When Jesus returns home to Nazareth in Mark 6, his townsfolk think he is only a carpenter. On two occasions, the disciples didn't grasp the implications of the feeding miracles. At the end of Mark they run away as the Jewish priests and elders sentence him to death—the disciples *never witness an appearance* of the resurrection. Simon Peter once thought he had figured out the mystery when acknowledging Jesus as the Messiah until Jesus told him the Messiah had to be crucified.[4]

The author offers the reason for the Jews (Jewish Christians) failing to see that Jesus was the promised Messiah, which he does through the secrecy motif—the revealing of Jesus as the Messiah was withheld from the Jews but open to the Gentiles (Hellenistic Christians, through Paul and Mark). Against all Jewish expectations, the Messiah was not about to destroy the national enemy; it would destroy him. Mark presents no birth story; his narrative begins with the baptism by John and Jesus having confirmation through a heavenly voice declaring him as the Son of God. A declaration occurs for three of the disciples (Peter, James and John) on the Mount of Transfiguration, and a final declaration is made at the cross by a Roman centurion (Gentile). Mark's Jesus was the Suffering Servant who became the Son of God at his baptism, not at his conception (as is found in Luke and Matthew), or at the beginning of creation (as is found in John).

Mark supports what theologians know as Adoption Christology, where Jesus becomes an *adopted* Son of God at his baptism. An adopted son in the Roman period may receive status. We imagine that adopted children today have lower status than those of their biological parents, but in the ancient world the reverse could be the case. Julius Caesar had two sons: Caesarion was his son, born of Cleopatra, his mistress, but Octavius had been adopted. Nothing of notice is known about Caesarion, but Octavian Augustus became the most powerful emperor of the Roman Empire. The contrasts between Augustus and Jesus—a Roman Emperor and a Jewish prophet—couldn't be more pronounced. The contrast is not insignificant in understanding how Paul's Radical Gospel was to be *received*.[5]

Conceptions of Jesus in the early sources of Paul in the 50s, and in Mark in the 60s, contrast sharply with the theology of John in the 90s:

> In the beginning was the Word, and the Word was with God, and the *Word was God*... And the Word became flesh and lived among us, and we have seen his glory, the glory as of a *father's only son*...
>
> Jesus said to them, 'Very truly, I tell you, before Abraham was, *I am.*'
>
> Whoever has *seen me has seen the Father*.[A]

Fourth-century Conceptions of Jesus

The contentious 'Arian Controversy' came to a head in the early fourth century at Nicaea in 325 CE. Arias had been an influential Christian from Alexandria who believed that 'Jesus was God'. He was aware that Jesus was the Son of God, but he also acknowledged that he must be God. For many Christians, it didn't make sense. It was confusing. If the 'Lord God' is Almighty, and the 'Lord Jesus Christ' is Almighty, surely, neither has a monopoly on might; neither can be ***All-mighty***! This led to disagreement and confusion amongst the Christian bishops. Arias claimed that *God and Christ existed before the beginning of time*, but God didn't become the Father until having the Son. He understood the personhood of Jesus Christ as a

---

[A] John 1:1–14, 8:58, 14:9

second-level divinity, who came into being, and who with the aid of his Father created the universe.

Bishop Alexander took exception to the teaching of Arias, even though it was popular in the churches at the time. For Alexander, *there was never a time when Jesus came into being*, because Jesus had always existed. The Son couldn't be second to The Father: *The Son was equal to the Father*. God the Father and God the Son were one and the same *entity*, and were co-equal. A Council of bishops was called in the eastern part of the Mediterranean, and the consensus of judgement sided with Alexander against Arias, and Alexander's view was formulated at the Council with the Nicene Creed.

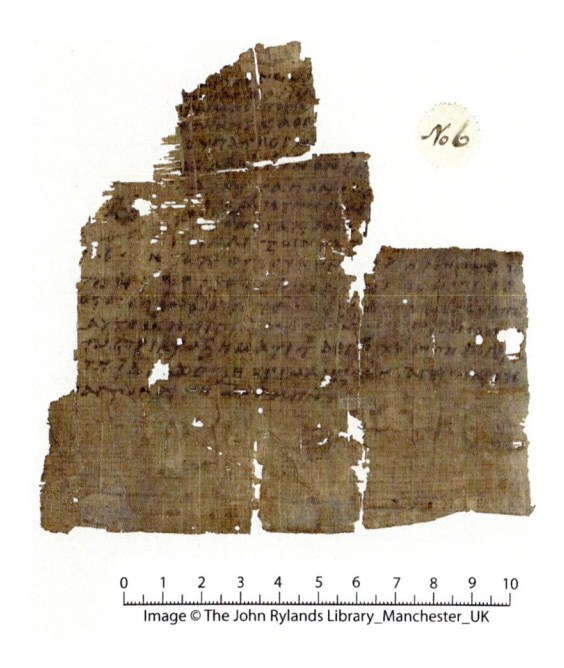

Oldest manuscript of the Nicene Creed (fifth century)

The issue at the Council was not to decide whether Jesus was God, but to define the *essence* or *substance* of Jesus, the Son of God, relative to God the Father. Every phrase of the Nicene Creed stresses the co-equality of the Son and the Father. The Creed confirms:

> One Lord, Jesus Christ, the only Son of God, was eternally begotten of the Father, God from God, light from light, true God from true God, begotten, not made, of one Being [*substance*] with the Father...

At the beginning of the second century, Ignatius writes of Jesus as God: 'Our God, Jesus: the Christ, was conceived by Mary'. And about Jesus he writes: 'God was manifest'.[6] But the different pictures of Jesus presented in Mark and the Nicene Creed are irreconcilable, as Bultmann observed:

> The formula 'Christ is God' is false in every sense in which God is understood as an entity which can be objectivized, whether it is understood in an Arian or Nicene, an Orthodox, or a Liberal sense...[7]

The Aramaic sources within the Synoptic Gospels uphold the assertion of Bultmann. There is no reference in the sources of Mark, Q., M., L., or Acts that claims that 'Jesus is God' (Chapter 7). A pressing question is how we get from A (Mark) to B (the Nicene Creed). The question of how the early Christians started to believe that Jesus was God requires a theory of the transition of Jesus—a Jewish prophet from Nazareth—becoming a divine Being, and which particular group of believers arrived at this transition.

The Transitional Divinity of Raymond Brown

The distinguished Roman Catholic theologian Raymond Brown posits a plausible account for the transition in thought from the early sources in Paul and Mark to the Nicene Creed of the mid-fourth century. Brown has addressed the question of how the first-century Jesus followers may have conceptualised the resurrection of Jesus. Would they not have reflected on his nature of being *alive again beyond the grave and sitting on God's right hand*? Wouldn't they have wondered about the point at which he became divine? We observe a trend of increasing divination of Jesus of Nazareth from the early to the late sources of the New Testament.

Would the followers of Jesus not have thought that, if Jesus was divine at his resurrection, he must have been divine throughout his ministry, from the day of baptism onwards? *Mark reflects this view*. Brown then argued that if Christians later believed that Jesus must have been divine from his baptism, he must also have been divine throughout his entire life. So they began telling stories about Jesus being born divine, which we find in the *birth narratives of Matthew and Luke,* where Mary conceives of the Son of God through the Holy Spirit. Christians may later have wondered that if

Jesus, the Son of God, was divine at conception, he must also have been divine from before creation, which we find in the *Prologue of John's Gospel*. Considering the more exclusive scope of the Jewish Christian mission as compared to the outreach of Paul and his associates, it seems more likely that Hellenistic Christians would have arrived at this perspective.

The Sacrament of the Last Supper, Salvador Dali, 1955

Christian Miracles

Ehrman postulates that conversions occurred because of a belief that the God of the Christians was *more powerful* than any other deity of Greco-Roman religion, which might be true, but it is conjecture. He also thinks that miracles were the major factor in conversion—not that 'God-fearers' had witnessed them personally, but that they'd heard of others who had, and believed their reports to be true. That again may be correct, but we have no way of knowing this either. For Christianity to succeed, Ehrman says, it had to be shown to be *more powerful than* the gods of paganism.[8]

The God of the Jews created the heavens and the earth, but the Christian God performs miracles. The Son of God cured the sick, exorcised demons and raised the dead, and although he was crucified as a criminal by the Roman prefect, his God could raise him from the dead to everlasting life. Apollo and Jupiter couldn't do that for Julius Caesar or Caesar Augustus; they were history before Saul of Tarsus came on the scene, recalled only by their annual festivals. Romulus ascended to heaven but couldn't avert the Civil War; Jesus ascended to heaven to establish the Kingdom of God. Augustus may sit on his throne in heaven as Jupiter, and talk through the thunder, but Christ is seated on the right hand of God to save Christians from the *wrath* to come, and to *raise the dead imperishable*. Could the dread of the imminent judgement have influenced the increasing conversions of God-fearers to Christianity?

New Testament Theology of Heavenly Powers

Michael Heiser writes extensively about a hidden realm of 'principalities and powers' in the cosmos of the biblical period, a background that has largely been overlooked in New Testament scholarship (apart from J.B. Caird's *Principalities and Powers* in 1956).[9] The biblical state of the world from the antediluvian period was corrupted and in need of redemption. For the Christians, this would occur when Jesus the Messiah returned to redeem the fallen state that led to the banishment of mankind from Eden. Heiser's thesis begins with the narratives of Genesis, 1 Enoch and Jude.[10] Heiser asked whether a mythical cosmology pervaded the consciousness of Jewish Christians, and latterly of pagan converts, in the first century.

We have seen how the first-century Jewish and pagan world was steeped in superstition; we noted that Octavian not only built temples to Roman deities, but also worshipped and offered sacrifices as an instinctive action before going into battle. It was inconceivable throughout the Empire that the populace at large would not have wanted the security of knowing the gods were on their side through their day, before life-changing decisions, or when facing major crises. The New Testament was the product of later Hellenistic Christians, and Jesus is presented in the canonical Gospels as having power over demons: Jesus experiences a mystical vision of Satan falling from heaven, and the temptation stories in the Judean desert have Jesus debating with the devil. Not only does John the Baptist prepare the Jews for the coming *wrath*, but also the New Testament is set upon such a foundation. There are biblical references to the judgement scene, and an apocalyptic upheaval in *heaven* and earth, of *forces above* and rulers below. Note how many allusions there are to a hidden world above. Paul writes:

> Neither death, nor life, *nor angels*, nor rulers, nor things present, nor things to come, *nor powers, nor height, nor depth*, nor anything else in all creation, will be able to separate us from the love of God...[A]

The letters to the Ephesians and Colossians refer to 'rulers and *authorities in heavenly places*', to '*cosmic powers*', and '*spiritual forces of evil in heavenly places*'. There must be a distinction between the earthly *and* the heavenly realms in terms of: 'all things in heaven *and* on earth', 'visible *and* invisible', 'thrones' *and* 'dominions', 'rulers' *and* 'powers'.[B] How should we interpret the *principalities* and *powers* in the heavenly places?

In Paul's first letter to the Corinthians, an allusion to 'fallen angels' of the antediluvian world is made. Paul thinks women converts ought to have a symbol of authority on their heads, '*because of the angels*,' a caution that is unintelligible outside a cosmology presupposed in the Genesis narrative of the 'Sons of God' (fallen angels) impregnating beautiful women.[11] Paul asks, rhetorically: 'Who will ascend into heaven?' (to bring Christ down), and 'Who will descend into the abyss?' (to raise Christ up).[C] The letters to Peter refer to the *'Spirits in prison'* and to fallen angels.[12] And:

> If God did not spare *the angels when they sinned*, but cast them into hell and committed them to chains of deepest darkness to be kept until the judgment... then the Lord knows how to rescue the godly from trial, and to keep the unrighteous under punishment until the day of judgment.[D]

These citations are echoes of the Genesis myth of the fallen angels ('Sons of God'), which portray a primitive cosmology of Hebrew thought. They are found in the books of Deuteronomy, Job, Daniel and the Psalms, and are reflected in 1 Enoch and the Dead Sea Scrolls:

[A] Romans 8:37–39
[B] Ephesians 3:10–11, 6:11; Colossians 1:16; 2:14–15
[C] Romans 10:6
[D] 1 Peter 3:19–22; 2 Peter 2:4–10 (Titus 3:1)

> God has taken his place in the divine council; *in the midst of the gods* he holds judgment: 'How long will you judge unjustly...?' I say, '*You are gods, children of the Most High*, all of you; nevertheless, you shall die like mortals, and fall like any prince.' Rise up, O God, judge the earth; for all the nations belong to you!^A

> When the Most High apportioned the nations, when he divided humankind, he fixed the boundaries of the peoples according to the *number of the gods;* the Lord's own portion was his people, Jacob his allotted share.^B

The most graphic apocalyptic references to an unseen heavenly realm are found in the books of Jude and Revelation:

> War broke out in heaven; Michael and his angels fought against the dragon. The dragon *and his angels* fought back, but they were defeated, and there was no longer any place for them in heaven...^C

> And *the angels* who did not keep their own position, but left their proper dwelling, he has kept in eternal chains in deepest darkness for the judgment of the great day... Enoch, in the seventh generation from Adam, prophesied, saying, 'See, the Lord is coming with ten thousands of his holy ones, to execute judgment on all, and to convict everyone of all the deeds of ungodliness that they have committed...'^D

Commentators have frequently interpreted the *principalities* and *powers* as human rulers and governors; that this can't be the case is evident by their inclusion *with* the earthly rulers. In addition to the many social benefits in converting to Christianity, and belonging to a closely-knit community, might a significant attraction be the idea of being 'put right' with the 'one true God' (becoming righteous), as opposed to feeling the need to placate oneself with an uncaring deity? Might the attraction of being saved from the *wrath* to come by the Messianic Lord, who loved them, and who gave his life for them, be a compelling attraction for Greco-Romans to embrace in the first-century cosmology of malevolent and uncontrollable powers?

A Psalm 82:1–6
B Deuteronomy 32:8–9
C Revelation 12:7–9
D Jude 1:6–16

The Problem of Miracles Today

If Christian conversion rates increased from paganism through miracles and fears of *wrath*, principalities and powers and fallen angels above in a primitive and superstitious cosmology, we are compelled to address the issues of authenticity in light of our modern understanding. Miraculous events beyond the laws of physics and natural causation are not part of a modern conception of how life functions, as was the case for those in the first century. The New Testament documents were conceptualised within a worldview of the miraculous, but this is not how most people conceive of reality today.

Paul says he could speak with tongues of angels (*glossolalia*) and perform *signs* and *wonders* by the power of the Spirit of God (though no accounts of his *signs* and *wonders* appear in his letters).[13] Luke has Paul throwing a venomous snake from his hand at Malta, without doing him any injury, Simon Peter healing a lame man and raising Dorcas from the dead, Philip disappearing from the Ethiopian eunuch, and the apostles receiving the Holy Spirit to enable them to heal and speak in foreign languages.[14]

We reach an impasse in our search for Paul in terms of miraculous events taking place, owing to the differing cosmologies of ancient and modern times. These are the pertinent facts: Jesus of Nazareth and Paul were said to have performed miracles according to our sources, but the nature of the sources renders them inadequate for an analysis of their authenticity. And yet Christian centres sprang up in major cities of Alexandria, Syria, Asia, Galatia, Achaia, Macedonia and Rome. This couldn't have occurred without a sizeable number of pagans converting to Christianity.

In Summary

The Radical Gospel of Paul wasn't an entirely novel teaching for a pagan world to embrace. The teaching of the crucified and raised Saviour of the World integrated within the mythological conceptualisation of the Greco-Roman world. In Jesus of Nazareth, God-fearing citizens were to identify with every Christian divine-human tradition. The Radical Gospel of Paul had resonance with the legends of Romulus and emphasised the contrast between a military Roman warmonger and a Jewish pacifist prophet.[15] A

Lucan tradition of the Holy Spirit overshadowing the virgin has parallels with birth legends of Hercules, but we find no beguiling deity disguised as a mortal being within the literature of the New Testament. The Word becoming flesh of John has no direct link with Roman mythology.

Mark's presentation of the ministry of Jesus was pedagogical. The voice of God heard *only* by Jesus at his baptism was recorded for the benefit of readers to illustrate who Jesus really was: that it was not meant to be for those present at the scene is evident from the fact that throughout Mark's Gospel no one seems aware that Jesus was the Son of God and the Jewish Messiah before the resurrection. The Transfiguration reminds the reader that the disciples did not understand who Jesus was, and would not have done, even if he revealed himself with two veteran prophets of Israel. We cannot interpret Mark's interventions of the heavenly voices as historical *events* without reference to the author's theological intentions.[16]

Jesus is never called God in the Synoptics, and even John's Gospel never portrays Jesus as claiming specifically that he was God.[17] The sermons of Peter and Paul, which Luke attributes to the beginnings of the Christian mission, do not speak of Jesus as God. Although Paul views the Christ of Christian faith as trans-personal, he falls short of equating Jesus as God.[18] There is no evidence of first-generation Christians conceiving of Jesus as God in the earliest strata of the New Testament tradition, even though it became the main topic of debate at the Council of Nicaea.[19] However, the conception of Jesus *becoming divine* (God manifest), as argued by Ehrman and Brown, parallels the mythological beliefs underlying pagan religion. How conversion rates had been influenced by miraculous performances is difficult to say. Although Paul's first letter to the Corinthians suggests that first-generation believers received the gift of the Holy Spirit, without details of a psychological nature of what occurred and how it occurred, it is not possible for the historian to make an informed assessment.

Notes

[1] As confirmed by Philo, Clement of Alexandria and Origen. Philo writes:

> When he [Moses] was about to depart from hence to heaven, to take up his abode there, and leaving this mortal life to become immortal, having been summoned by the Father, who now changed him, having previously been a double being, composed of soul and body, into the nature of a single body, transforming him wholly and entirely into a most sun-like mind. (Philo: *On the Life of Moses* 2.51.288)

2   Isaiah 44:6, 45:1–7. It is unclear in this text why a King of Israel was addressed as 'God' (*elohim*) when Isaiah 44:6 claims there is only one *Elohim*. *Elohim* is one of a number of Hebrew nouns that sometimes take plural *-im* (masculine plural) and *-oth* (feminine plural) endings with singular verbs, adjectives and pronouns to indicate majesty or greatness. There are a few cases where idols are called 'gods' in the Hebrew Bible, e.g. Psalm 82:6.

3   Luke and Paul not only reflected early Christological formulations, they went beyond them. Their theological conceptions transferred from what Jesus was at the resurrection to what he had always been (at conception / at creation), a perception obscured from his disciples and the Jewish nation in the ministry. Paul knew Jesus was a Jewish prophet, 'born of a woman', but viewed the Christ of Christian faith as a divine being. Mark's Jesus became the Son of God at baptism, and an early codex of Luke completes Psalm 2: 'You are my Son, *Today* I have begotten you' (other sources of Luke omit 'Today', but in Acts Luke viewed the resurrection [not the baptism] as the fulfilment of the Psalm). Matthew and Luke follow Mark in time, and for both (particularly Luke) the divinity of Jesus occurs at conception (immaculate conception by God with a virgin). This was known as *Incarnational Christology*. A decade later when the Gospel of John appeared, the divinity of Jesus was understood to have occurred before creation.

4   Mark anticipates the end of the Jewish nation, when the Temple would be destroyed. The Jewish War marks the beginning of the end. The Son of Man was at the gate ready to make his appearance. Those who were ashamed of Jesus' words would be put to shame when the Son of Man arrived; those who accepted his words and became his followers would then enter into glory. Ehrman summarises the theology of Mark: 'Mark's story of Jesus is replete with paradoxes: the glorious messiah is one who suffers an ignominious death; exaltation comes with pain, salvation through crucifixion; to gain one's life one must lose it; the greatest are the most humble; the most powerful are the slaves; prosperity is not a blessing but a hindrance; leaving one's home or field or family brings a hundredfold homes and fields and families; the first will be last and the last first. These lessons provide help for a community that is in the throes of

suffering, experiencing the social disruptions of persecution. They make particular sense for a community that knows that its messiah, the Son of God, was rejected and mocked and killed, only to be vindicated by God, who raised him from the dead' (Ehrman 2012: 102-103).

5 Adoption Christology was the earliest understanding of how Jesus came to be seen, but there were other Christologies. One Christian sect thought that Jesus and Christ were two distinct *entities*, that Jesus, the Son of God had two natures: body and Spirit. They taught that he never suffered on the cross, but only *seemed* to suffer: they were called *Docetists*. Other Christian sects believed that Jesus was born human but Christ entered into him at baptism and departed when his body deceased on the cross: they were called *Separatists*. Other Christianities formed ideas that had an internal logic, such as *Modalists*, who argued that a person could be understood in different modes of being (one can be a son to his father and at the same time the father to his son, a teacher to his pupils etc.). But this didn't make sense for many; it implied singularity when everyone accepted that Jesus and God *couldn't be the same entity*: Jesus prayed to his Father, not to himself. These Christologies were rejected, but they were attempts to understand how a human being could become divine. Tertullian coined the doctrine of the Trinity that temporarily settled the matter.

6 Brown 1957: 568 (Ignatius: *Ephesians* 18:2; 19:3).

7 Bultmann 1955: 273–290.

8 Ehrman 2018: 131–159. Wright (2018) departs from his professed role as a historical critic in failing to face up to the dilemma of miracles in relation to our modern understanding of the world. He tends to accept biblical miracles at face value: 'One person's miracle is another person's magic', he writes (Wright 2018: 127), whatever that might mean. He puts down the releasing of Peter's shackles in prison at Philippi (Acts 16:25–26) as merely an earthquake (2018: 182), which is fanciful (this was not Luke's intention), and rather than accept that Paul had a mystical vision at Troas calling him to depart from his planned itinerary and go into Macedonia (Acts 16:7–10), he spends not a few pages arguing that other (more sociological) factors were involved. Wright seems reluctant to question the text or to apply any discrimination in relating an author's intention when applying his source traditions. He admits that the account on Malta was no doubt compressed and idealized: Wright 2018: 383. The record of Paul's voyage

to Rome is implausible: Paul takes charge, gives advice, and predicts that all will be saved from shipwreck: Wright 2018: 375.

9   Heiser 2015; 2017.

10 The *Book of Enoch* was widely known amongst the Jews in the first century, and a version was found amongst the Dead Sea Scrolls. The story of Enoch provides the context (Genesis 1:1–6:4) of the Flood Story (Genesis 6:5f), which is derived from Mesopotamian traditions widely known, and which comes in many versions. The contrast between the Hebrew story of Noah and the Mesopotamian story of Gilgamesh (Utnapishtim etc.) centres on the purpose and cause of the flood (see Chapter 9). The books of *Enoch* and *Giants* were widely known amongst literate Jews, and are cited in the Dead Sea Scrolls.

11 1 Corinthians 11:10 / Genesis 6:4. Heiser 2017: 123–144. Paul is not concerned about nature, but about cosmic boundaries; that women without their heads covered would be at risk of sexual violation by the fallen angels of Genesis 6:4. It had happened once before (Genesis 6:1–4): Heiser 2017: 135.

12 The '*Spirits in prison*' goes back to the pre-Flood, and the fallen 'sons of God' of Genesis 6:1–4: Heiser 2017: 138–142.

13 Acts 3:1–10, 9:36–42, 28:3–6. There are references to Paul preforming miracles in three authentic letters: 'I *speak in tongues* more than all of you.' (1 Corinthians 14:18); 'Christ has accomplished through me to win obedience from the Gentiles, by word and *deed*, by the *power of signs and wonders*, by the *power* of the Spirit…'. (Romans 15:17–19); 'My proclamation was not with plausible words of wisdom, but with a *demonstration* of the Spirit *and of power*.' (1 Corinthians 2:4); 'Signs of a true apostle were performed among you with utmost patience, *signs* and *wonders* and *mighty works*.' (2 Corinthians 12:12)

14 Luke's narrative of Peter converting Cornelius is unconvincing if what Paul writes in Galatians is accepted: the testimonies are inconsistent.

15 The military figure of Christ found in the Christian book of Revelation was to battle with the reigning kings of the earth before the final battle of oblivion, a vastly different image from the Gospel person of Jesus (Revelation 19:11–21).

16 Brown 1994: 85–86.

17 The use of *theos* for Jesus, which is attested in the early second century, was a continuation of an application that began in the New Testament period. The

Christian formula, 'Jesus is Lord', gave Jesus the title *Kyrios*, which is the standard translation for Yahweh in the Greek Septuagint: Brown 1957: 566.

18 This negative conclusion is substantiated by the fact that Paul doesn't use the title in any passage before 58 CE. Paul's first occurrence of 'God' for Jesus is in Romans:

> They are Israelites, and to them belong the adoption, the glory, the covenants, the giving of the law, the worship, and the promises; to them belong the patriarchs, and from them, according to the flesh, comes the Messiah, who is over all, God blessed forever. Amen. (Romans 9:5)

Brown says: 'If we could be certain of the grammar of this passage, we could thus date the usage to the late 50s': Brown 1957: 566. Traditional scholars cite Romans 9.5b as the prime New Testament text which refers to Jesus as 'God'. But it is debatable since it involves a grammatical problem in the koine Greek. The problem is in ancient Greek. When Paul wrote in the first century, Greek was like many other ancient languages, in having no punctuation, no spaces between letters, and all letters in capitals: *uncials*. Punctuation, spaces and upper/lower cases were not incorporated into Greek until centuries later. NT grammarians agree that a correct translation of Romans 9.5b cannot depend on a Greek grammar that didn't exist back then. The question about how to interpret Romans 9.5b can be stated as follows: in accordance with later, punctuated Greek, should a colon or full stop be inserted after the word *sarka* ('flesh') in the unpunctuated Greek text? In either case, the independent clause begins after it, a doxology to God the Father, and the clause does not call Christ 'God'.

19 'He [Jesus] never indisputably uses of himself the title "the Son of God"': Brown 1994: 89. The Gospel of John was written to manifest Jesus as the Son of God (John 20:31). 'My father' never appears in Mark and is applied only four times in Luke. Matthew's uses of 'my Father' have no Synoptic parallels (Mark 3:35 and Luke 8:21 compared with Matthew 26:29). Matthew uses 'my Father' in texts which first lacked the designation: Brown 1994: 85.

7

Contradictions in the Gospels

The Gospel of Paul

Paul refers to only *one* Gospel (singular) in his letters.

> I want you to know, brothers and sisters, that *the Gospel* that was proclaimed by me is not of human origin.
>
> Paul, a servant of Jesus Christ, called to be an apostle, set apart for *the Gospel* of God...[A]

There could only be *one* Gospel for the apostle Paul, and yet there are four in the New Testament (four 'The Gospel According to...'). Why believers in Jesus settled on four accounts of a ministry of Jesus is unclear, but for research into the historical Jesus it presents a dilemma. Historians taking an interest in the historical Jesus, as the first-century Jewish prophet from Nazareth, are required to examine all available source material, but for a good many practising Christians such an exercise is not considered to be expedient to faith. When historians study anyone of antiquity they search for sources which are consistent, with only minor variations in detail, but this is not what they find in the canonical Gospels.[1]

Mythicists who examine the Gospels for the historical Jesus (Robert Price and Richard Carrier), and atheistic publicists (Christopher Hitchens and Richard Dawkins), who require tangible evidence, have drawn attention to the contradictory details in the Gospel narratives.[2] The problem cannot be pushed aside if Christianity — which emerged from historical events in time and place — is to remain credible and meaningful.

[A] Galatians 1:11; Romans 1:1 (*My Gospel*: Romans 2:16, 16:25)

Second-century Christian bishops became increasingly nervous about the appearance of so many pseudonymous Gospels: the *Gospel of Thomas*, the *Gospel of Philip* and the *Gospel of Truth*, to recall just three. What solutions did they come up with? One was the solution of Marcion in the 140s and have only one Gospel (Luke and ten letters by Paul: Marcion disregarded the Old Testament altogether), but a Roman bishop excommunicated him for heresy. Another was to harmonise the *memoirs* of Jesus into a coherent account, which is what Tatian carried out in *c.* 165. These two solutions have been applied since, particularly the method of harmonisation.

We must confront the evidence and accept that—whether by providence or serendipity—we have four accounts of the ministry of Jesus which are inconsistent. What sense do we make of the contradictions in the Gospel accounts? In this chapter we highlight some obvious contradictions and inconsistencies in the Gospel narratives after looking at the nature of the earliest manuscripts we have available.

Source Transmission

There is a consensus amongst critical scholars that the canonical Gospels are not independent of one anther. There was copying of early tracts of the Gospels during the first century. The consensus amongst the critics is that Matthew and Luke used Mark as their primary source, that Matthew and Luke used another (unknown) source independently of one another, and that John used a unique source, and may have had access to Synoptic material, primarily Luke. Critical scholarship can only go on the evidence available. There may be fresh discoveries in the Egyptian soils—a buried pot with unknown Gospels—that require a revised hypothesis of textual analysis, but at this point in time scholarship can only go on the evidence available. If this conclusion is correct, it has to conform to the will of God (for fundamentalist Christians) that we have four *bona fide* accounts of the historical Jesus in the New Testament which are not independent.

Let us review the evidence of textual copying of our early manuscripts in possession. Statistical analysis illustrates that 97% of written narrative in Mark is found in Matthew and Luke, and 52% of this material is repeated verbatim.[3] The source common to Matthew and Luke, which is not found in Mark, is known as the Q Source, or the *Gospel of Q*. Matthew and Luke have extra material unique to each of them: these are called the M. and L. Sources respectively. This Synoptic Gospel source theory is plausible and accounts for the data, but still remains supposition, since no such sources have been found. Scholars have argued that this is not to be unexpected, since there would have been no necessity for early Christians to preserve material that was incorporated in the Gospels of Matthew and Luke.[4] In addition, the evangelists were not eyewitnesses of their source material. Apart from the textual ambiguities in the Gospel narratives (which imply that pre-existent pericopes were put together), Luke's opening dedication states explicitly that the author had not been an eyewitness. Later copies of Mark have material by later scribes (three or four appearance stories of Jesus to the disciples) which aren't found in the earliest manuscripts. The final edition of John preserves two conclusions, which points to editorial redaction, and there are inconsistencies in time and location in chapters 3 to 5, which suggests an editor had rearranged an earlier version of John.

The combined evidence suggests that the canonical Gospels in circulation today have been the product of editorial reworking during transmission. The earliest codex of Mark available has been dated to 220 CE, 150 years after it was written. The earliest combination of the four Gospels (in the order of Matthew, John, Luke, Mark, followed by Acts) is dated to *c*. 250.[5]

Chester Beatty codex P45 (*c*. 250 CE, part of Luke's Gospel)

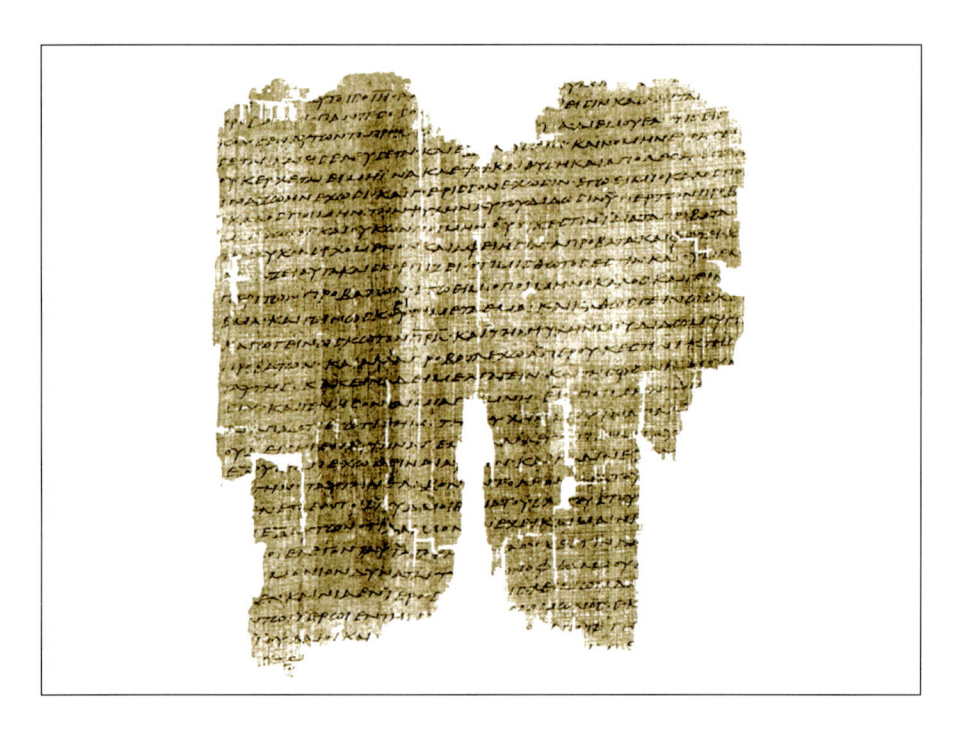

Chester Beatty Papyrus 1 (Matthew 20-21, 25-26; Mark 4-9, 11-12; Luke 6-7, 9-14; John 4-5, 10-11; and Acts 4-17)

A scholar named John Mill devoted 30 years of his professional career in 1707 to analysing the early manuscripts in possession. He had available about 100 manuscripts at the time. This was the age of the printing press, and a decision had to be made for the most accurate text for printing. He painstakingly arranged the whole New Testament in columns, word-by-word in sentence-by-sentence formation, and in each column he recorded and counted all alternative renditions, and found there were over 30,000 variants in the manuscripts.[6] Mill demonstrated that *no manuscript of the early period was word for word identical.*

John Mill was criticised for subverting Holy Scripture, but his supporters rallied to his defence and said that he was only recording *what was in the manuscripts*. Today we have more than 5,700 copies, or part copies, of the New Testament, which is 57 times more than were available to John Mill (scribal variants are published in the margins of the modern study Bible). How can we know what Mark first wrote? We can't; we can only claim we have a gist of what the author of the Gospel of Mark reported of what

Jesus had spoken and done. If historians want to know what Mark wrote, and we have more than 5,700 early copies of Mark, they have a dilemma.

Most textual variants in the early manuscripts are quite insignificant and rarely alter the meaning of a given text, but they haven't been preserved inerrant through providence. There is an argument that in light of every available manuscript variant being so minor the canonical Gospels are to be accepted as containing authentic data on the historical Jesus.

Contradictory Details in the Gospels

The Gospel of Mark begins with the baptism of Jesus in Jordan by John the Baptist. John takes his readers to the beginning of time. Matthew and Luke have genealogies of Jesus' ancestry, which are contradictory.

1. Matthew has the father of Joseph as Jacob, the son of Matthan, but Luke has the father of Joseph as Heli, the son of Matthan. Was the grandfather of Jesus, then, *Jacob* or *Heli*? It depends on which Gospel is prioritised.
2. Did Joseph and Mary come from *Bethlehem* or *Nazareth*, and travel to Bethlehem for the Roman census? The accounts differ.
3. When Jairus left home in Mark to find Jesus, *his daughter was alive*. In Matthew *she had already died*. Who was correct?
4. Did Jesus curse a fig tree *on the morning* he entered the Temple, or did he curse it *the following day*? Mark and Matthew don't agree.
5. During the trial in Mark when Pilate asked whether Jesus was the king of the Jews, his only response was, 'Your words'. But, in John, *Jesus engages in an extensive philosophical dialogue*. Which account is the most dependable, Mark or John?
6. Was Jesus crucified from *9.00 am on the 15th Nissan*, Passover day, or from *12.00 noon on the 14th Nisan*, the Day of Preparation? Mark and John have different calendar days and time periods.
7. Did Jesus *carry his own cross*, or was he *assisted by one from the crowd*? It all depends on which Gospel is read.
8. The details covering the events of the crucifixion, and the resurrection *do not cohere* historically.

According to Mark, as Jesus is being mocked by 'bystanders, chief priests and scribes' with crucified criminals beside him, *he says not a single word* until giving up his last breath, in which he calls: 'My God, my God, why have you forsaken me? (*Eloi, Eloi, lema sabachthani?*)

According to Luke, Jesus stops along the road and says to his mourners:

> Daughters of Jerusalem, do not weep for me, but weep for yourselves and for your children. For the days are surely coming when they will say, 'Blessed are the barren, and the wombs that never bore, and the breasts that never nursed.' Then they will begin to say to the mountains, 'Fall on us'; and to the hills, 'Cover us.' For if they do this when the wood is green, what will happen when it is dry?

On the cross, Jesus cries: 'Father, forgive them for they don't know what they are doing.' Only one convict mocks Jesus; his fellow scolds him and asks Jesus in turn to remember him when he comes in his kingdom. Jesus said: 'Truly I tell you, today you will be with me in Paradise'. Jesus takes his final breath and cries: 'Father, into your hands I commend my spirit.' Luke *has no Cry of Abandonment* (the only Saying reported in Mark).

What were the final words given by Jesus: just the desperate expression reported in Mark, or the Sayings in Luke? John records different Sayings: a commission for the 'disciple whom Jesus loved' to take in his mother; 'I am thirsty,' and 'It is finished.'

Is the solution to harmonise the Gospels? Consider the resurrection texts:

1. How many women visited the empty tomb: just one, Mary Magdalene, or three named women?
2. Did an earthquake roll away the stone as the women arrived (as said in Matthew), or had it already been moved (as said in Mark)?
3. What did the women find: one young man, an angel, or two angels (was one of them Jesus?)?
4. Were the women instructed to tell the disciples that Jesus would meet them in Galilee (Mark)? Or were they told not to leave Jerusalem, where Jesus would meet them (Luke)?
5. Did the women say nothing (Mark), or did they tell the disciples

(Luke, John); did Jesus meet the disciples (Matthew), or did Jesus meet only Mary Magdalene (John)?

The answers depend on *which Gospel is given priority*. The problem with harmonising the Gospels is that their theological perspectives are often overlooked in the interests of trying to force the accounts to fit together. We are ignoring the inherent contradictions that exist in the texts.

Addressing the Contradictions

Suppose the evangelists were not so much interested in history as in the *meaning of history*. And suppose they were in receipt of variant sources through oral and written traditions that weren't identical in some minor details. Suppose, also, that much information regarding the ministry was unknown, such as what went on during the trial, or the Sayings of Jesus on the cross. What do we think the evangelists could have done with the source material? The question cannot be answered through blind faith, but by examining the data. Christianity is about a spiritual relationship, not about textual analysis of the Gospels, or the historicity of Jesus.

Whilst the four Gospels in sum record historical events, the data shows that the way the evangelists applied their material suggests their primary interest was more theological than historical. Let us review some of these contradictions and ask whether a theological point is being made in the way each evangelist has used his source material.

Birth Narratives

Beginning with the genealogies, which evangelist may have redacted his source for a theological purpose? Luke says he 'investigated everything carefully from the beginning' to compile 'an orderly account', but when we read Matthew, we notice that Joseph has an instruction from an angel on three occasions through a dream. Can we recall a patriarch who had been derided as the *dreamer*, whose father was Jacob? Our minds go back to Joseph, father of 'the children of Israel'. The question to ask is whether Matthew's readers were intended to make the connection of Joseph, the father of Jesus, with Joseph (re-named Israel), son of a Hebrew patriarch.

Did Matthew modify his source (from Heli to Jacob) deliberately for such a theological purpose?

Looking at Matthew again, we see a connection between the 'slaughter of the innocents' in Bethlehem by King Herod and the killing of the Hebrew babies by the Pharaoh: this was to form a theological connection between Jesus of Nazareth and Moses, who gave Israel the Law. Matthew has five blocks of teaching (the first on a mountain) where Jesus was presented as the new Lawgiver to supersede Moses, who was believed to have written the five books of the Pentateuch. This cannot be incidental.

Miracle Stories from Mark to Matthew

We begin with the healing narrative of Jairus' daughter. It is evident that Matthew intensified the miracle stories he had found in Mark. Matthew appears to have redacted the miracle stories of Mark, shortening them by removing their descriptive details, but intensifying their overall effects. Study Mark's miracle narratives that are duplicated in Matthew and note the pattern. Although it seems surprising to modern ears, the miracles of Jesus make no impact upon the disciples. When Matthew applies Mark's narrative of Jesus walking on water, for example, he has the tradition of *Peter also beginning to walk on water* before starting to sink, an event which evokes a confession of faith. The disciples worshipped Jesus and confess: 'Truly, you are the Son of God.'[A] Mark's application of the miracle stories serves a different theological purpose.

Compared to Mark, Matthew seems quite lenient with Peter. When Peter makes his confession at Caesarea Philippi, Jesus scolds him in Mark, yet when Matthew uses the story, he gives Peter the elevated position as the founder of the Church, a status not granted in Mark.[B] Matthew and Mark applied the miracle traditions to expound different theologies. Mark puts the disciples down, but Matthew less so.[7]

[A] Matthew 14:22–33 / Mark 6:45–58
[B] Mark 8:27–33 / Matthew 16:23–24

Mark presents Simon Peter negatively, Matthew treats him gently, John gives him a hard press compared to 'the disciple whom Jesus loved', but Luke gives him the highest status. It seems as though the miracle sources of Jesus are more theologically determined than historically represented, and that the profile of Peter in the Gospels is confused and unhistorical.

The Crucifixion

What of the crucifixion narratives in the Gospels? Why do we have such stark contradictions in the accounts of the same event? The riddle of the Messianic secret in Mark has been the subject of longstanding discussion amongst scholars. Why does the Jesus of Mark keep informing recipients of healing to keep their recovery secret? It seems as though Mark's Jesus wanted his identity as the Messiah and Son of Man undisclosed until the disciples had realised that as the Jewish Messiah he had to be crucified. Did the historical Jesus teach in such a coded way? I suspect not. It was Mark's way of explaining why the Jews failed to recognise Jesus as their Messiah. Mark presented Jesus as a *Suffering* Son of Man who offered his life as a ransom for humankind:

> **The Son of Man came** not to be served but to serve, **and** to give his life as a ransom for many.[A]

Luke presents Jesus as an *ideal martyr on the road to Jerusalem*:

> When the days drew near for him to be taken up, he set his face to go to Jerusalem. And he sent messengers ahead of him. On their way they entered a village of the Samaritans to make ready for him; but they did not receive him, because his face was set toward Jerusalem.[B]

Jerusalem was central to Lucan theology. The disciples were instructed not to leave Jerusalem at the resurrection, they received the Holy Spirit in the *city of Jerusalem*, and it was *from Jerusalem* that the Gospel spread into the Gentile world, but not before the Jews had rejected the message of Jesus. Luke takes the incident of Jesus returning home to Nazareth from Mark

---

[A] Mark 10:45
[B] Luke 4:24, 9:51–56, 13:33–34, 18:31, 19:28

and modifies the sequence of events by bringing it forward to follow the story of the baptism, so as to stress the (Jewish) rejection of Jesus' mother and siblings, and fellow villagers of his upbringing.[8]

Luke's Jesus was initially rejected by the Jews of his *hometown*, then Jews of the *city of Jerusalem* (taunting crowds at the trial) and finally by *national opposition* as the Gospel spread abroad into the wider world. The Gentiles received the Gospel because the Jews *refused* the invitation of Jesus. This is not history, but a different theology to that of Mark.

Matthew follows Mark in respect of the crucifixion narratives, but John puts the crucifixion back to when the Paschal lambs were being sacrificed in the Temple: twice in John's Gospel, John the Baptist announces Jesus as 'The Lamb of God'. And finally, soldiers at the foot of the cross did not break his legs, so that his bones would not be broken, a detail that recalls the Passover lamb, which was to have no injury or blemish.[9]

The evangelists adjusted their sources in line with their agendas of how Jesus of Nazareth (and redemption) was to be viewed. The Gospels texts cannot be harmonised effectively without distorting their meaning and misrepresenting the intention of each evangelist. The crucifixion of Jesus has been verified historically, but the accounts of Jesus' crucifixion in the Gospels cannot be relied on as an authentic record of what had actually taken place. The Gospels of John and Luke have no dereliction of Jesus: 'Why have you forsaken me?'. Mark's Jesus was tormented by the ordeal, but this was not the case for Jesus in Luke, or John. The Johannine Jesus, particularly, remains in control of the drama that has to be played out.

The evangelists represented Roman officials positively and the leaders of the Jews negatively, which can hardly be historical. Theological motives have guided the presentation of *Rome as innocent* and the *Jewish nation as guilty* for the death of Jesus: compare the behaviours of Pilate with those of the elders, the chief priests and the Jewish crowds in the four Gospels. A transition has occurred because the evangelists were writing at a time when Christians felt it expedient to curry favour with Rome to forward the cause, thereby modifying their traditions from a Palestinian setting of the early 30s to a Greco-Roman one of their current day.

When Richard Carrier critiques the Gospel accounts, he points to various historical improbabilities in the Gospel narratives.[10] When Jesus calls the first disciples, they leave the nets and boats of their livelihoods to follow a complete stranger! First-century fishermen of rural communities would not behave in such a way. Jesus is transported through mid-air, speaks to the devil on a pinnacle of the Temple and walks upon water, three stories which deny the laws of physics. Can the modern reader be expected to swallow this? Was Jesus a Harry Potter? The disciples come over as naive and dumb—they witness a multitude feasting on tiny quantities of food, but a day or so later enquire how it might be possible to feed such a vast crowd. Jesus withers the fig tree for having no fruit when it was *not the season to produce ripe figs*. The Jews require Judas Iscariot to identify Jesus when he had just entered the city of Jerusalem amidst a thronging crowd and caused a disturbance in the Temple court. Hundreds of Jews, and the armed patrol of police looking out for potential rioters, seem completely unaware of the disruption in the Temple. Matthew writes about corpses coming out of their tombs when Jesus had died. Mark's three women rise early in the morning to embalm Jesus' corpse, but have no idea how they could enter a tomb that they had witnessed was sealed two days earlier.[A]

But the Gospels are not biographies of a life of Jesus: they are theological, not historical, *reflections*; they are *interpretations* of the ministry; they are theological *perspectives*, not historical certainties. When the two accounts of Mark and John of Jesus' agonising prayer in the garden are contrasted, it will be seen that there's no *agony* in John and no *garden* in Mark.

Analysis of the Arrest of Jesus

What differences stand out between the accounts in Mark and John of the arrest of Jesus?[11] Mark's Jesus prays alone in agony: 'I am deeply grieved, even to death… If it's possible, let the hour pass from me.' This is not the case for John. After Peter is ordered to put away his sword, Jesus says: 'Am I not to drink the cup that the Father has given me?' The tormented Jesus of Mark *throws himself to the ground*, whilst an authoritative Jesus of John *remains standing on his feet* and the band of soldiers *fall to the ground*.

[A] Mark 1:16–20, 6:35–44, 45–52, 8:1–40, 11:1–26, 14:10–44, 16:3; Matthew 4:5, 27:52

Consider the terminology applied in the Gospel of John over the arrest of Jesus. We notice that the 'band'/'detachment' (Greek: a *spira* or *speira*) of soldiers was sent to arrest Jesus. The term *spira* represents a cohort of 600 legionaries, a tenth of a legion in full compliment. Their 'captain'/'officer' (Greek: *ciliarsis*) would lead the Tribune of troops. The Jewish authorities appear to have brought along the entire military defence of Jerusalem to arrest Jesus (a military captain with 600 armed soldiers). *They all fall to the ground before an unarmed Jewish pacifist!* Was this historical, or Johannine hyperbole? Theologically, the narrative is full of significance in respect of *power and authority*. Consider the prayer of Jesus in these two references.[12]

Mark's Jesus pleads *let the cup be taken away*. John's Jesus *takes the cup*:

> And what should I say—'Father, save me from this hour?' No, it is for this reason that I have come to this hour.[A]

In Mark, the disciples desert Jesus and run away, 'to fulfil Scripture'. The Jesus of John orders the armed guards to let his disciples go, 'to fulfil the word he had spoken' (Jesus, according to John, is the Word become flesh, which is tantamount to the word of Jesus being Scripture[B]). We have the Scriptures predicting the flight of the disciples and another their release:

> 'Let the scriptures be fulfilled.' All of them deserted him and fled. (Mark)

> 'Let these men go.' This was to fulfil the word that he had spoken, 'I did not lose a single one of those whom you gave me.' (John)

What historical sense can we make of the accounts of the arrest of Jesus? They are different theological constructions, two different pictures that can be summarised in these two Sayings:

> My God, my God, why have *you deserted me*? (Mark)

> *I am not alone* because the Father is with me. (John)[C]

[A] John 12:27
[B] John 1:14
[C] Mark 15:34; John 16:32–33

For this reason they are called Gospels, and not Histories or Annals. The four accounts of Jesus in the Gospels are separate reflections, complete in themselves, composed by authors who would not expect their writings to be compared or contrasted with any other versions.

Notes

1. See my book: *You Say That I Am* (Lines 2017).

2. Carrier 2014; Dawkins 2016; Hitchens 2008; Price 2000.

3. Stein 2001: 37; Farmer 1976: 208-209; Ehrman 2012: 88-153. Of 11,025 words found in Mark, 132 have no parallel in either Matthew or Luke: 97% of Mark is in Matthew, and 88% is in Luke, compared to less than 60% of Matthew is duplicated in Mark, and only 47% of Luke is found in Mark.

4. Classically referred to as the Synoptic Thesis. The Synoptic Thesis argues for the priority of Mark over Matthew and Luke. Given that so much material in Mark is common to Matthew and Luke, and that the pericopes are more vivid in colour and content, it is speculated that Matthew and Luke have used Mark as their primary source. There is no doubting the interdependence of the Synoptic Gospels, but there are scholars who do not accept this hypothesis. Mark is clearly writing for a Gentle community, which is why in Mark 7:1-4 the author needs to explain Jewish customs. We note also a primitive nature in Mark's source material: for example, the few Aramaic terms found in Mark (*Ephphatha, Talitha cum, Corban*) are not in Matthew, which suggests the latter is dependent on the former: Ehrman 2012: 105-113.

5. The Chester Beatty codex known as P45 (Chester Beatty 1): Hurtado 2006: 34.

6. Ehrman 2005: 83-88.

7. Jesus said:
   'Why are you talking about having no bread? Do you still not perceive or understand? *Are your hearts hardened? Do you have eyes, and fail to see? Do you have ears, and fail to hear*? And do you not remember? When I broke the five loaves for the five thousand, how many baskets full of broken pieces did you collect?' They said to him, 'Twelve.' 'And the seven for the four thousand, how many baskets full of broken pieces did you collect?' And they said to him, 'Seven.' Then he said to them, '*Do you not yet understand*?' (Mark 8:17-22)

8. I have examined this Marcan narrative in *You Say That I Am* (Lines 2017).

9. John records:
   One of the soldiers pierced his side with a spear, and at once blood and water came out. (He who saw this has testified so that you also may believe. His testimony is true, and he knows that he tells the truth.) *These things occurred so that the*

scripture might be fulfilled, 'None of his bones shall be broken.' (John 1:29, 36, 20:33-34)

10   Carrier 2012; 2014.

11   **The arrest of Jesus according to Mark**:

He took with him Peter and James and John, and *began to be distressed and agitated. And he said to them, 'I am deeply grieved, even to death*; remain here, and keep awake.' And going a little farther, *he* **threw himself on the ground** and *prayed that, if it were possible, the hour might pass from him*. He said, 'Abba, Father, for you all things are possible; **remove this cup from me**; yet, not what I want, but what you want.'... 'Have you come out with swords and clubs to arrest me as though I were a bandit? Day after day I was with you in the temple teaching, and you did not arrest me. **But let the scriptures be fulfilled**.' *All of them deserted him and fled...* (Mark 14:32-53).

The arrest of Jesus according to John:

After Jesus had spoken these words, he went out with his disciples across the Kidron valley to a place where there was a *garden*, which he and his disciples entered. Now Judas, who betrayed him, also knew the place, because Jesus often met there with his disciples. So Judas brought *a detachment of soldiers* together with police from the chief priests and the Pharisees, and they came there with lanterns and torches and weapons. Then Jesus, **knowing all that was to happen to him**, came forward and asked them, 'Whom are you looking for?' They answered, 'Jesus of Nazareth.' Jesus replied, 'I am he.' Judas, who betrayed him, was standing with them. When Jesus said to them, 'I am he,' *they stepped back and fell to the ground*. Again he asked them, 'Whom are you looking for?' And they said, 'Jesus of Nazareth.' Jesus answered, 'I told you that I am he. So if you are looking for me, let these men go.' **This was to fulfil the word that he had spoken**, 'I did not lose a single one of those whom you gave me.' Then Simon Peter, who had a sword, drew it, struck the high priest's slave, and cut off his right ear. The slave's name was Malchus. Jesus said to Peter, 'Put your sword back into its sheath. **Am I not to drink the cup that the Father has given me?**' So *the soldiers, their officer, and the Jewish police* arrested Jesus and bound him. First they took him to Annas, who was the father-in-law of Caiaphas, the high priest that year. (John 18:1-13)

12   Ehrman 2012: 243. J.D. Crossan and J. White: *Alpha and Omega Ministries* (2014) Debate: 'Is the orthodox and biblical account of Jesus of Nazareth authentic and historically accurate.'

8

Forged Christian Documents

Forgery in the Ancient World

The Roman physician, philosopher and author Galen overheard two men arguing about a book he had written in a market store (they disagreed on the authorship of the book), and so he wrote another book with the title *On His Own Books*, so that buyers would recognise the work as one of his. Whether the story is apocryphal or not, it makes the point that authors in antiquity were just as worried about forgery as authors are now. Forgery became a problem in Christianity when it became a religion informed by books, and forged Gospels by characters in the ministry began to appear.

There were no means of checking the authenticity of books purported to have been written by the apostles of Jesus after the first witnesses passed away. The New Testament contains documents that critical scholars now believe were not written by the names ascribed to them. They used to be called 'pseudepigrapha', but today they are regarded as forgeries.[1]

Christian Forgeries

The canonical Gospels all have anonymous authors: their names are not recorded on the early manuscripts. The titles (Matthew, Mark, Luke and John) were the product of second-century guesswork. There were other Gospels that were supposedly authored by Peter, Philip and John (son of Zebedee), and by the brothers of Jesus, James and his twin Thomas.

French archaeologists excavating a cemetery at Akhmîm in 1886 found a codex of the *Apocalypse of Peter* in the coffin of a Christian monk. Grenfell and Hunt discovered papyri fragments of previously unknown Gospels at Oxyrhynchus in 1896, and, finally, an eastern vegetable farmer named Muhammed al-Samman dug up thirteen leather-bound codices of vellum at Nag Hammad, Egypt, in 1945. These codices of early papyri fragments were probably hidden away in periods of Christian censorship. The non-corrosive elements of Egyptian sands in cemeteries and rubbish tips have yielded a rich repository of early manuscripts.

Other Gospels have since been discovered, such as the *Gospel of Mary*, the *Gospel of Magdalene*, the *Gospel of Nicodemus* (or the *Acts of Pilate*) and the *Gospel of Judas*. Codices of other Acts and Letters composed (allegedly) by the apostles have emerged. The authenticity of early writings supposedly written by men and women cited in the ministry cannot be authenticated without internal or external evidence: the majority were forgeries.

The *Apostolic Constitutions* was a Christian document that proved to be a forgery. Scholars have estimated the date of composition as around 380 CE. It was believed to be a collective document of the apostles describing how the Church should be organised: who led the churches, what should be their qualifications, and how baptism and Eucharistic services were to be carried out. The pseudonymous authors all speak in the first person. The *Constitutions* concludes with a warning for Christians *not to read books that are falsely claimed to be written by the apostles*. Why would the imposter say this? It was probably because he did not want readers to suspect him doing what he had done. He was trying to divert potential doubters from being suspicious. So, Christian forgers were thereby condemning forgery early on! One giveaway clue to a document being forged is a *paradoxical proof*—a familiar trait of an author or request of a colleague: 'I, Paul, write this with my own hand'; 'Bring me the cloak I left with Carpus at Troas'; 'Eubulus sends you greetings'.

Forged Documents in the New Testament

Most Christian forgeries were not included in the New Testament canon, but some were, forged in the sense that the manuscript ascriptions aren't authentic. The *Gospel of Peter* is included in two early canons of Scripture, but nowadays is believed to be apocryphal. The discovery at Akhmîm by French archaeologists contains fragments of a 66-page anthology, part of which includes forgeries by Simon Peter (*Gospel of Peter* and *Apocalypse of Peter*). Eusebius of Caesarea (260-340 CE) knew of the *Gospel of Peter*.[2]

The apocryphal *Gospel of Peter* was by an unknown author in the second century when Peter would have been dead for 60 years: it was a forgery. The *Gospel of Peter* appears in two early versions, both in the first person: the canonical Gospels are not written in the first person.[3] The *Apocalypse of Peter* presents guided tours of heaven and hell. The chosen ones are in heaven and have pure white skin and pale complexions, flowers are open in full bloom and everyone joins in choral prayers throughout eternity.

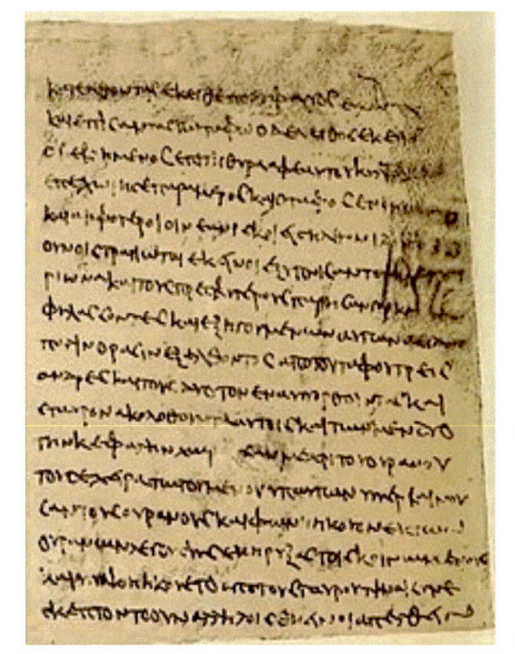

Coptic Text of the *Gospel of Peter*

Oxyrhynchus, Nag Hammadi and Akhmîm in Egypt

The damned in hell are suspended by parts of their body over the *Lake of Bubbling Mire*: adulteresses are roped by their locks of hair; adulterers are roped by the feet with their heads over the *Mire*; murderers, transvestites and lesbians are driven over a cliff by the angels to be tortured forever by grotesque creatures, images recalled by Dante and Hieronymus Bosch.

An Angel Leading a Soul into Hell, Hieronymus Bosch, 1450-1516

The Letters of Peter

1 Peter

There are a few other works ascribed to Peter besides the above, and the pressing question is: does the New Testament contain books named after Simon Peter that are widely considered to be forgeries? Two letters in the New Testament refer to Peter as the author (neither is in the first person):

> Peter, an apostle of Jesus Christ, to the exiles of the Dispersion in Pontus, Galatia, Cappadocia, Asia, and Bithynia...[A]
>
> Simeon Peter, a servant and apostle of Jesus Christ...[B]

The author of the first letter of Peter testifies to himself as an apostle and a witness to 'the sufferings of Christ', a claim unfounded in the Gospels.[C]

[A] 1 Peter 1:1
[B] 2 Peter 1:1
[C] 1 Peter 5:1

Suffering is the major theme of the letter: 1 Peter refers to suffering more than any other book of the New Testament, including the Gospels. What form of suffering the author was referring to is unclear.[A]

A traditional view was that it reflected the political persecution by Rome, as occurred in 64 CE when Nero blamed Christians for setting the city of Rome on fire, but there is nothing in the letter that indicates the nature of suffering to which the author was referring.[4] The context suggests it may have been quarrels and fallouts amongst relatives and former friends due to the altered lifestyles required when joining Christian *ecclesias*.

Christian converts took no part in Roman festivals and ceremonies, and meetings were often convened in hidden places, but such covert activities led to suspicion by the authorities and social isolation of the converted. An author asked that his readers should be 'obedient to the government', and of 'good conduct', and to be dutiful slaves, wives and husbands.[B] An exhortation was drawn from the Septuagint version of Hebrew Scripture, indicating that the author was conversant in Greek. The conclusion says the letter was written *through* 'Silvanus', which could mean that Silvanus was a courier, or that he was known by the *ecclesia* as a 'model Christian'.

The first letter to Peter is addressed to 'exiles of the Dispersion in Pontus, Galatia, Cappadocia, Asia, and Bithynia', which suggests the church was situated in a city of Turkey. The reference to Babylon is interesting: 'Your sister church in Babylon… sends you greetings.'[C] Christians at the end of the first century identified Rome as Babylon. After the fall of Jerusalem to Babylon in the sixth century BCE, it became synonymous with all Jewish enemies. Such a reference presupposes a church setting largely of Gentile converts somewhere in Turkey after the Jewish War in 66–70 CE (it is pro-Christian and anti-Semitic). If the early tradition is right that Simon Peter was martyred in Rome in 64, he couldn't have been the author of 1 Peter. But there are other reasons to doubt Petrine authorship of 1 Peter.

[A] 1 Peter 4:12–13
[B] 1 Peter 2:13–15, 18–3:7
[C] 1 Peter 5:13

The Calling of Saints Peter and Andrew, Caravaggio, 1603

2 Peter

The second letter of Peter has a different literary style and content to the first letter. The author identifies himself as 'Simon Peter', as the disciple who witnessed the Transfiguration.[5] The second letter has no reference to suffering of any form, but mounts an attack on the 'destructive heresies' and particular opponents said to be 'licentious, greedy and exploitative'. No specific information of what heresies or opponents is given, however. In addition to *false teachers*, the author is critical about 'scoffers' mocking the teaching that Jesus would soon return.[A]

The writer also says his work was in agreement with the writings of Paul, whose work he regards as Scripture, but Paul's letters were not classified as Scripture at the time of Peter, and neither had they been put together. Simon Peter, Paul and the early Christians had been convinced that Jesus

---

[A] 2 Peter 3:8

would return in their day (at the *Parousia*), 'within this generation', and before the twelve disciples had 'tasted death', in the words of Mark.[A] The second letter was written well after the death of Simon Peter.

Could Simon Peter Write in Greek?

Whoever wrote the two letters of Peter was clearly conversant in Greek. Most critical scholars are convinced the historical Simon Peter could not have written 1 and 2 Peter, for the reason that *Simon Peter would not have been able write*.[6] Empirical studies in social anthropology have shown that only 3% of the Jewish population in Palestine in the first century would be able to read, and a smaller percentage would be able to write books or letters. Simon Peter had been a peasant fisherman from a Galilean hamlet called Capernaum, whose native tongue was Aramaic, not Greek.

Reading and writing had been taught separately in the ancient world, not together, as they are today. The art of writing documents was the reserve of the educated classes from large cities where there were formal schools. The first letter of Peter is in a sophisticated form of rhetorical Greek, but Peter lived from coastal fishing, and would have had limited resources to have attended school. It is possible that Peter received a formal education after the resurrection of Jesus, and that he engaged on a language course in classical Greek and rhetorical composition. But is it actually plausible, particularly if he had a family of young children to support? Luke in Acts claimed that *Peter and John were illiterate*.[B] Commentators have suggested that Peter may have enlisted someone to write on his behalf, but there are no examples in the ancient world of anyone from a low-class background purchasing an amanuensis, whereas there are at least two books ascribed to Peter that could not have been written by him. Writing in the name of Simon Peter seems to have been a cottage industry at the close of the first century. Although an imposter would want others to read his work, if he were unknown it would be unread. However, if the book were written in the name of Simon Peter, not only would devout believers read it, but it might get classified as Christian Scripture.

[A] Mark 13:30; 9:1
[B] Acts 4:13

Pseudonymous Christian Documents

A pseudonymous document is a work of an author whose name is found on a manuscript, but whose identity is unknown in relation to anyone of note (e.g. an apostle, or person mentioned in the Gospels). The document cannot be viewed as 'pseudepigrapha', because the author hasn't alleged to be someone other than who he was.

The author of James was not the brother of Jesus: he never claimed to be the brother of Jesus (the New Testament mentions six men called James). Martin Luther thought the letter was an 'epistle of straw', and denied the apostle James was the author on the grounds that: a) the content was in conflict with Paul's teaching on justification through faith, and b) it made no reference to the crucifixion and resurrection of Jesus. Commentators generally believe the letter of James reflects the conventional morality of early Jewish Christianity. It has been dated from the late first to the early second century: the earliest manuscript dates from the mid-third century.

A further pseudonymous document is the letter of Jude. According to the Gospel of Mark, Jesus had a brother named Jude, but the author does not refer to himself as a relative of Jesus: he says he was a 'brother of James', but which James is not mentioned.[A] The author of the book of Revelation referred to himself as John, but John was a common name in Palestine.

Authentic Letters of Paul

According to a majority of critical scholars, of the thirteen books ascribed to Paul in the New Testament, only seven are authentic to him: they are 1 and 2 Corinthians, Galatians, Philippians, 1 Thessalonians, Philemon and Romans.[7] I summarise below how such a conclusion has been drawn. We consider the three pastoral letters of Timothy and Titus, 2 Thessalonians, and finally the more disputable letters of Ephesians and Colossians.

1 Timothy

Timothy was a colleague of Paul, whom he left behind to be the leader of a church at Ephesus. The author, claiming he was Paul, instructs Timothy

---

[A] Mark 6:3

about running the church, telling him to sort out teachers who propound absurd theories of 'myths and genealogies', and ascetic lifestyles, such as anti-marriage and strict dietary restrictions. He was to ensure the correct members were appointed for the duties of bishops and deacons: namely, married *men*, who had been converted for some time, and who had lived virtuous lives. Rules were prescribed for newly converted women. They must be *subject to,* and must have *no authority over, their male brethren*, for example, by teaching: they were to *remain quiet in the ecclesia*. An analogy from the Adam and Eve tradition was given to illustrate the appropriate status of gender relationships. Women could be saved, not by the death and resurrection of Jesus (as Paul had said), but through 'childbearing'.[A]

2 Timothy

The author of the second letter to Timothy (also alleged to be Paul) was in prison in Rome (no location is given for 1 Timothy). Paul was waiting for his second trial (*soon*) before being condemned to death. He expresses love and concern for Timothy, and that he hoped to be reunited with him in Rome before the arrival of winter, and that he would wish Timothy to bring along with him the cloak he left behind at Troas.

Titus

The contents of the letter to Titus and first Timothy are strikingly similar. Paul (the alleged author) writes to Titus instructing him to sort out those teachers who promoted 'false teachings', 'genealogies' and 'mythologies'. In an identical style to that found in the first letter to Timothy, the author outlines the conducts required of old brothers and sisters, young brothers and sisters, and Christian slaves in the *ecclesia*.

Assessment of the Pastoral Letters

The three pastoral letters of Paul have been thought to be forgeries from 1807, following the pioneering examination of Sliermarcher. Sliermarcher argued that the pastoral letters commonly use words and develop ideas which are at odds with those found in the authentic letters of Paul.[8] And further, the false teachers the author criticises are not dissimilar to those holding doctrines we now term *Gnostic*. The introductions in both letters

---

[A] 1 Timothy 2:11–15

to Timothy are virtually identical, but are nowhere else repeated in such a form in the authentic letters. The pastoral letters also have clauses (the 'promise of life', 'with a pure conscience', 'from a pure heart', and 'God the deposit [of faith]'), which are not in common with Pauline thought.

The British critical scholar A.N. Harrison published a complete appraisal of the pastoral letters in 1921.[9] He produced statistics about word usage and observed that 848 different terms are used in the pastoral letters, and of that number 306 were used by Christian authors of the second century. He also illustrated that common terms employed by Paul in the authentic letters are used differently in the pastoral letters.[10] When Paul contrasts the Gospel with 'works of the law' in the letters to the Galatians and the Romans, he was clearly referring to those Jewish regulations of the Torah (circumcision, kosher and Sabbath), but the 'good works' of the pastoral letters referred to charitable deeds.

There are other contrasts. Paul advises unmarried converts in the *ecclesia* at Corinth to remain single (as himself) in preparation for the coming of the Lord, but in the pastoral letters the forger instructs church leaders to be married. Women, he wrote, were to be saved by bearing children, not through the death and resurrection of Jesus (as Paul had said).[A] The three pastoral letters presuppose an *ecclesial* context which is highly structured and orderly.[B] The setting of the Corinthian *ecclesia* by contrast had been a lax and informal community practising gifts of the Holy Spirit (to teach, heal and speak in angelic tongues) so that the whole *ecclesia* could benefit as an organic unit; it was non-hierarchal and was anything but orderly![C]

Everybody in Christ was equal, male and female, slave and master, Jew and Gentile, but the churches of the pastoral letters reflect congregations which are hierarchical and regimented.[D] Inevitably, there resulted chaos in the Corinthian *ecclesia* and a complete lack of order: infighting, taking brethren to court, and disputes over moral and ethical issues (whether to eat meat sacrificed to pagan idols, whether the resurrection was *physical*,

---

[A] 1 Timothy 22:2
[B] 1 Thessalonians 4:14–18
[C] 1 Corinthians 12–14 (12:13)
[D] Compare with Galatians 3:28

or whether it was right to sleep with one's stepmother). To address such issues, Paul appealed to the *ecclesia* as a whole, and to individuals within it, not to 'leaders' ordering them to discipline errant believers, since there were no such leaders appointed by Paul. The pastoral letters allude to a later situation than the period of Paul. They were forgeries written in the name of Paul for Hellenistic converts encouraging them to conform to the teachings of the apostles.[11]

2 Thessalonians

A dominant tone in the first letter to the Thessalonians is of an imminent *Parousia,* and the consequences for those believers who had fallen asleep. Paul provides Thessalonian believers with an assurance that just because a few of their brethren had died it didn't mean they wouldn't receive the reward of resurrection. They were to be raised from the dead to greet the Lord in the air (what theologians call the rapture), after which those alive would be rescued from the *wrath* of God's judgement. Paul thought that that Jesus would arrive in his own day:

> *We who are alive, who are left* until the coming of the Lord, will by no means precede those who have died. For the Lord himself... will descend from heaven, and the dead in Christ will rise first. Then *we who are alive, who are left, will be caught up in the clouds* together with them to meet the Lord in the air; and *we* will be with the Lord.[A]

The analogy of a pregnant woman is given to illustrate the suddenness of the day of the Lord's arrival. Although, reasons Paul, a pregnant woman knows she'll have her baby, the time of birth cannot accurately be known beforehand; it will occur unexpectedly, as a thief breaking in at night.[B]

We do not find any such urgent expectation of the end time in the second letter to the Thessalonians, quite the reverse. The author wishes to correct a misconception in the first letter by dampening down any expectation of an imminent coming of the Lord. He virtually declares that Paul had not written a previous letter to the church. 'Let no one deceive you,' he says,

---

[A] 1 Thessalonians 4:17
[B] 1 Thessalonians 5:2

'for that day ***will not come*** *unless the rebellion comes first*'.^A The *end time is not quite so near.* Certain events must first take place, such as upheaval on the earth, and the Antichrist taking his seat in the Jerusalem Temple and declaring himself to be God:

> And then the lawless one will be revealed, whom the Lord Jesus will destroy with the breath of his mouth, annihilating him by the manifestation of his coming.^B

Allegory of the Apocalypse, Joseph Heintz the Younger, 1674

'There seems to be a fundamental disparity between the teachings of 1 and 2 Thessalonians', concludes Ehrman.[12]

A 2 Thessalonians 2:2
B 2 Thessalonians 2:3–8

The author claims he had *already told them* 'these things' when he was last with them. In which case, we ask, what sense should we make of the first letter? The second letter to the Thessalonians suggests that Paul had not spoken about a *Parousia* beforehand. The unanticipated *suddenness* of the *Parousia* has evaporated into a series of observable signs, and the sense of imminence of a catastrophic and *not quite so near* event occurring on earth has become a programme of calculation in preparation for a long haul of history. And so the forger is critical of sloth and idleness, saying that it is unacceptable for Christians to avoid work on the basis that the coming of Jesus is just around the corner.

The closing greeting of 2 Thessalonians is the giveaway to the letter being a forgery.[A] The forger offers *paradoxical proof* of authenticity:

> I Paul, write this greeting with my own hand. This is the mark in every letter of mine; it is the way I write.

The *paradoxical proof* implies that 2 Thessalonians wasn't dictated (as was normal by the use of an amanuensis). It could be counter-argued that the letter was indeed authentic and that the signature was *proof* of Paul being the author (the traditional view), rather than it being the means by which a forger was offsetting a presumption that the letter might be questioned. But, no *proof* of identity is found in any undisputed letter of Paul (it may be argued that Galatians ends with a similar note: 'See what large letters I make when I am writing in my own hand.').[B] A *paradoxical proof* can only make sense if the forger was trying to convince readers that he was Paul, but it shouldn't be the only criterion in judging authentic authorship. On balance, it seems that 2 Thessalonians had been a forged letter of Paul to account for a delay of the *Parousia*. It was produced by a Christian scribe, who wanted his readers not to neglect their daily duties in Christian life.[C]

Ephesians and Colossians

The letters of the Ephesians and the Colossians have similar themes, and critical scholars remain divided over the authenticity of their authorship.

[A] 2 Thessalonians 3:17
[B] Galatians 6:11
[C] 2 Thessalonians 3:6–12

Conservative scholars see them as characteristic of Pauline theology, but radical scholars do not agree; there has been a move towards a sceptical position of Pauline authorship of both books in modern times, owing to their different theological perspectives compared to what is found in the authentic Pauline letters.[13] Freddie Bruce argued that the letters perfectly summarise the more refined theology of Paul, but liberal scholarship has recently disputed this view.[14]

The major contentions centre on whether Paul changed his views as time went on, owing to a delay of the *Parousia*. Comparing the urgent tone of expectation of the *Parousia* in 1 Thessalonians with the *experience of living* in 'heavenly places' in the letters to the Ephesians and Colossians, we can draw only one of two deductions: a) that they were by different authors, or b) the same author wrote them, but altered his views as time went by.

Ephesians

Bruce believed that Paul wrote the letter to the Ephesians ('He thought it encapsulated better than any other letter the heart and soul of Paul's theology'), but the critic Christiaan Beker disputed his thesis in 1970, in a comprehensive study of Pauline theology.[15] Beker believed that Paul had not written the letter to the Ephesians for the following reasons.

The contents of the letter to the Ephesians sound like Paul, he contended, but when one digs deeper differences and discrepancies start to appear. The letter to the Ephesians was designed to remind the Gentiles of their alienation from the Israelite God and the Jewish hope of reconciliation.[A] Converts had now been put 'right with God' (become righteous), and the barrier that divided pagans from Jews (i.e. the Torah) was now removed through the blood of Christ, the point being that Jewish and Gentile Jesus believers can now celebrate together in Christian unity. Theology covers the first two chapters before ethics point to how the Ephesians were to live in unity in Christ Jesus.

Beker showed that the literary style of the letter to the Ephesians was not typical of Paul's writing. Sentence constructions in the authentic letters of

---

[A] Ephesians 3:1

Paul tend to be short and pointed, but the letter to the Ephesians has long complex sentences (nine have over fifty words).[A] There are many words in the letter that don't otherwise occur in Paul's genuine writings, but the principal reason for rejecting Pauline authorship is that the central motifs of Christian redemption are not consistent with what Paul had written in the authentic letters. According to the letter to the Ephesians, the author includes himself as one who was carried away by the 'passions of flesh': this is not like Paul. In the letter to the Philippians, he boasts about being 'blameless' and 'righteous' in observance of the Torah (Jewish Law), and he also talks about salvation 'apart from the works of the law' in his letter to the Romans, but in the letter to the Ephesians the author speaks about salvation apart from doing 'good deeds'.[B]

Another difference centres on suggestions that a Christian is *already saved* by God's grace, whereas when Paul uses the verb 'saved' in the authentic letters he always refers to the future. In other words, *salvation was not the reward that the Christian already has*; it is what a Christian *will have* when Jesus arrives in the clouds to rescue her or him from God's *wrath*.[C] One way to resolve the question of whether Paul modified his views as time went on is to compare the themes in Paul's early letters (1 Thessalonians, 1 Corinthians) with those in the later letters (such as Romans). According to the letter to the Romans, the believer has died through baptism to the 'powers of the world that are aligned with the enemies of God'. He never argued that believers would be raised in some form of *mystical union* to be with Christ, but that they would rise through baptism in *anticipation* of the personal resurrection at the *Parousia* (1 Thessalonians, 1 Corinthians and Romans).[D] God hasn't made the Christian *alive together with Christ* in some mystical sphere of *resurrection* in the 'heavenly places' (as written in the letter to the Ephesians), but will raise them *physically* from the dead at the general resurrection on the last day (as in 1 Corinthians).[E]

[A] Ehrman 2011: 110
[B] Ephesians 2:1–10/Philippians 3:4
[C] 1 Thessalonians 4:13–5:11
[D] 1 Thessalonians 4:13–18; 1 Corinthians 15:20–28; Romans 6:1–4
[E] 1 Corinthians 15:35–55/Ephesians 2:6

In point after point, the theology of the letter seems at odds with Pauline theology. It was written by a late Christian scribe in one of Paul's *ecclesias* to deal with a troublesome issue of his own day over Jewish and Gentile relations. It was written in the name of Paul by a forger who believed his motive could be justified, but he was knowingly composing a document that in time would be included in the New Testament as a letter of Paul.

Moreover, Luke's account of Paul's activity at Ephesus in Acts is open to question. The constitution of Christian *ecclesias* governed by 'elders' (say at Ephesus) is historically suspect, claims Bornkamm. Paul says nothing about this in the authentic letters. The overseers (*episcapi*) of 'the flock of Christ appointed by the Holy Spirit' reflects the latter-day Church in the time of Luke rather than the early period of Paul: the authentic letters say nothing about the Pauline *ecclesias* being governed by elders.[16]

Colossians

There is no consensus amongst commentators about whether the letters to the Ephesians and Colossians were composed by the same author. The author of the letter to the Ephesians may have used the Colossians letter as his major source, even though they have different agendas. The author is troubled about some (unidentified) promoting a heretical 'philosophy'. Regrettably, the type of philosophy is not specified, but it had something to do with the 'worship of angels', self-denial, food and drink obligations of Judaism, and attendance at religious festivals (the readers would have been aware of the context).

The author emphasises that only Christ is worthy of communal worship, not angelic beings, and that his death put an end to following the Torah. As in the letter to the Ephesians, the author believes that Christians have *been raised to be with Christ* in a cosmic *mystical union* in the here and now, but it does not imply that they have licence to live immoral lives, and so the last chapters cover the ethical demands of Christian living in Christ.[A] The German scholar Walter Bujard carried out a comprehensive study of the letter to the Colossians 40 years ago and analysed all the grammatical features of style (conjunctions, infinitives, participles, relative clauses and

---

[A] Colossians 2:6–19

streams of genitives) in the letter to the Colossians compared to those of the authentic letters of Paul (1 Thessalonians, Galatians and Philippians). Bujard showed that the style of writing contrasts sharply.[17]

Since the author also talks about the present experience of being raised with Christ in a *mystical state of experience,* the same argument applies to the letter to the Colossians as to the letter to the Ephesians: that the letter to the Colossians was by an impersonator in a different setting from that of Paul's day.[A] The forger was familiar with Paul's teaching, and in a few cases adopted Pauline phraseology, but notice that gender equality is not included in the reference from the letter to the Colossians compared with the authentic original in the letter to the Galatians:

> There is neither Jew nor Greek, there is neither slave nor free, there is no *male and female*, for you are all one in Christ Jesus.
>
> There is not Greek and Jew, circumcised and uncircumcised, barbarian, Scythian, slave, free; but Christ is all, and in all.[B]

Motives for Christian Forgery

Up to one third of the documents in the New Testament are anonymous or pseudonymous. Why would Christian authors forge documents of the New Testament and claim they were someone other than who they were, given that Christians emphasised the importance of the truth? It could be because they believed there were particular situations which warranted a half-truth, or even a lie, and believed it justifiable to present themselves as an authority when addressing an important issue. Plato acknowledged that physicians occasionally lied to get patients to take their medicines by saying they would otherwise not survive; and generals falsely promised their dispirited troops that reinforcements were soon to come to lift their morale to confront a more powerful army.

A Christian scribe could have felt so compelled to make his stand on an issue of religious principle that he falsified his identity by claiming to be

---

[A] Colossians 2:12–13
[B] Galatians 3:28; Colossians 3:11 (hence Colossians 3:18)

someone other than who he was. Other forgers may have wanted erring converts to conform to the *right teaching* against an erroneous philosophy. Another motive for some advocates of a radical teaching may have been to create a fictitious document in the name of a well-known authority to convince impressionable believers to accept their point of view. We know that first-century Christianity was anything but a homogeneous religion in practice and belief (in spite of claims by Luke). Could these instances have been motives for some Christian forgers to write in the name of the apostles Peter or Paul?

Notes

1   Ehrman 2012.

2   The third page of the Gospel of Peter begins mid-sentence and reads: '… and none of the Jews wanted to wash their hands, so Pilate stood up!' (The *Gospel of Peter*). The introduction recalls Matthew's comment of Pilate washing his hands. The Gospel follows the typical Passion narrative and includes an account of the resurrection. It is more anti-Semitic and more Docetic than the canonical Gospels.

> The night in which the Lord's day dawned, when the soldiers were safeguarding it two by two in every watch, there was a loud voice in heaven; and they saw that the heavens were opened and that two males who had much radiance had come down from there and come near the sepulchre. But that stone which had been thrust against the door, having rolled by itself, went a distance off the side; and the sepulchre opened, and both the young men entered. And so those soldiers, having seen, awakened the centurion and the elders (for they too were present, safeguarding). And while they were relating what they had seen, again they see three males who have come out from the sepulchre, with the two supporting the other one, and a cross following them, and the head of the two reaching unto heaven, but that of the one being led out by a hand by them going beyond the heavens. And they were hearing a voice from the heavens saying, 'Have you made proclamation to the fallen-asleep?' And an obeisance was heard from the cross, 'Yes.' (The *Gospel of Peter* 35–43)

The end of the *Gospel of Peter* has been lost after the text: 'I, Simon Peter and my brother Andrew decided to go fishing, and with us went Levi the son of Alpheus, whom the Lord…'. The author identifies himself as Simon Peter. The canonical evangelists don't disclose their names (the names attributed to them are no more than second-century guesswork based upon flimsy foundations, such as the account by Papias): Lines 2017: 367-368; Eusebius, *Ecclesiastical History* 3.39: 3–4.

3 Schleiermacher 1807, cited in Elliott 1993: Ehrman 2012: 94–97.

4 The Fire of Rome: Tacitus, *Annals XV* 44: Nero fastened the guilt and inflicted the most exquisite tortures on a class hated for their abominations, called Christians by the populace. Christus, from whom the name had its origin, suffered the extreme penalty during the reign of Tiberius at the hands of one of our procurators, Pontius Pilatus...

5 2 Peter 1:17/Matthew 17:1-8. The praising of Paul, and other features suggest late composition—this is not how Peter is represented in Galatians in relation to Paul (2 Peter 3:15-16/Galatians 1:6-2:14). 1 Peter views himself as a servant and elder, and a father to Mark (was this to connect with the author of Mark?). 1 Peter links with texts of Peter and Jesus: 'flock' resembles closing statements given by Jesus to Peter in John 21 (1 Peter 2:6, 13, 18; 3:1-7; 5:12).

6 Ehrman 2012: 70-73; Harris 1989.

7 The conclusion of Conzelmann (1976: 155) and Kümmel (1974: 141).

8 Ehrman 2012.

9 Harrison 1921.

10 'Faith', for instance, was used in Romans and Galatians to refer to trust in Christ for salvation, but 'faith' in the pastoral letters is a corpus of teaching: Titus 1:13.

11 Wright acknowledges that we don't have evidence of Paul writing the letter to the Hebrews, but he seems reluctant to accept that the disputed Pauline letters are forgeries under the name of Paul. It is perhaps regarding the pastoral letters that Wright finally faces up to the historical ambiguities. The second letter to Timothy claims to be written from Rome between two formal hearings; Paul had been supported by Onesiphorus, his friend from Ephesus, who came to Rome, searched for him and found him. This detail contrasts with the claim that 'all who are in Asia' have turned away from him (as written in 2 Timothy 1:15). Where is Timothy? He can't be in Ephesus if he needs Paul, in Rome, to tell him what's happening there. And where has Paul been? He writes about leaving his cloak at Troas, which would fit in with his earlier trip from Corinth to Jerusalem; but if he had wanted to send someone to retrieve his cloak, 'he would have been far more likely to do that from his two-year imprisonment in Caesarea than have to wait until he was in Rome'. He writes of sending Tichicus to Ephesus, which

could only work if the letters to Ephesians and Colossians were both written from Rome, not Ephesus, which would create further historical inconsistencies. He also sends greetings to Prisca and Aquila, but they are supposed to be in Rome after the edict banning all Jews from Rome under Claudius had been overturned. He writes that Erastus stayed in Corinth, whereas in Acts 19:22 he goes straight on ahead of Paul to Macedonia. He mentions leaving Trophimus behind in Ephesus, but in Acts 19:29 Trophimus was still with Paul in Jerusalem. So, if the second letter to Timothy is genuine, then it implies further activity of Paul in the East, but Acts has Paul under house arrest in Rome awaiting trial, and possible persecution under Nero. According to the first letter to Timothy, Timothy is in Ephesus. Paul gave him instructions about his work there, but there is little to connect the letter with Paul, 'or indeed with Timothy either'. Hymenaeus and Alexander are cited as blasphemers who were 'handed over to the Satan', but Hymenaeus crops up in 2 Timothy 2:17 with Philetus, this time over a charge of 'saying that the resurrection has already happened'. It is a puzzle, he says. As for the letter to Titus, the problems are compounded: Luke in Acts 21:1-3 has a different itinerary than that in Titus: Wright 2018: 284-286.

12   Ehrman 2012: 107.

13   Most critics think it improbable that Paul wrote the letter to the Ephesians: these include Brandon, Beare, Bultmann, Conzelmann, Dibelius, Goodspeed, Moffatt, Nineham, Pokorny, Schweizer and Weiss. Modern critics include Ehrman and Crossan, but not Bruce, Goulder nor Wright. Raymond E. Brown reports that 80% of authoritative scholars today don't attribute either letter to Paul, seeing the author as Deutero-Pauline. Some manuscripts omit the parenthesis ('in Ephesus') in the introduction of Ephesians 1:1. This suggests it may have been a circular letter. Marcion thought Ephesians was addressed to the church at Laodicea.

14   Wright (2018) accepts both letters as being genuinely authored by Paul when he was imprisoned at Ephesus in 55/56. Objections based on differences in style, he claims, can be said about 1 and 2 Corinthians: Wright 2018: 303-305.

15   Beker 1980; Ehrman 2012: 109.

16   Bornkamm 1971: 98.

17   Ehrman 2012: 113; Koester 2000 (48 words are use in Colossians that are nowhere else found in the genuine writings of Paul).

9

Towards a Theology of The Bible

A Revised Theology of the Bible

The Christian Bible is generally discarded in the secular world of western democracies. This is because it supports a cosmology and worldview that is outmoded, largely irrelevant as a teaching tool for moral conduct, and because it has stories which are unpleasant, to say the least, and difficult to defend (the book of Revelation has some of the most violent images of the Bible). Simple answers will not do. Some bypass the problem through diversion, and filter out the stories of immoral conduct; others will argue the Old Testament presents the tribal, violent Jewish God, and the New a loving Father of Jesus, but both options do not stand up to scrutiny. The second option fails to recognise that both Testaments contain theological and ethical difficulties, and it fails to appreciate the relationship between them both. Christianity grew out of Judaism, and has antecedents in the Hebrew Scriptures. The Old Testament has considerable insights, and the New Testament has sources that we might consider are problematic. For Christianity to stand up against modern criticism, a revised theology of the Christian Bible is called for, otherwise it will be reduced to forms of superficial secularism, or be sabotaged by fundamentalist agendas.

During religious development, I was encouraged to search for the *Golden Thread of God's plan of Salvation* from Genesis to Revelation. I was to study the prophetic books of Scripture for forecasts and 'signs of the times' of a coming Kingdom of God, but the evidence of an ancient book serving as an almanac for divining future events is not credible. After two millennia with no hint of a second coming of Jesus and history being wound up, is it still feasible to apply scriptural forecasts in such a way, in spite of what the historical Jesus or Saul of Tarsus may have believed during the 30s? The case for a revised theology of the Christian Bible is presented in this last chapter, but first I show why it is so imperative to carry out the task.

Abuse of the Bible

Should Christian Scripture be studied as a series of prophetic predictions of the coming of Jesus, or proof texts condemning the Jews for rejecting Jesus as the Son of God and Jewish Messiah? Can evangelists go on using the Bible as the manual of *truth* to denounce Muslims, or to promote the *correct beliefs* against Christians of a different tradition of faith?

Unsavoury Stories in the Bible

How should the impartial reader make sense of those stories in the Bible, such as Joshua massacring *every* man, woman and child, and animals, of Jericho? Can the sacred impulse of Jephthah sacrificing *his own daughter* to honour a vow ever be justified? Is it commendable by modern ethical standards to legitimise such behaviour because it conforms to the will of God? Is it morally acceptable for a deity *to visit the iniquity of the fathers on the children* to the third and fourth generation? Can we really applaud the righteous indignation of Samuel when *cutting up a foreign king into pieces* 'before the Lord'? Can we accept the tradition of the prophet Elisha and the *42 boys mauled to death* by two bears for making fun of his baldness—an incidental detail passed by with no critique by the author?[A]

Were these gruesome deeds really applauded by Yahweh, the God of the Jews, or did biblical authors *interpret* them this way? If they are assessed as appropriate for the ancient world, what importance are we to give to the Bible today? In what sense should we now regard it as God's word?

Venerated heroes of Israelite history were endorsed by their chroniclers because their religiosity conformed to what they believed to be the will of God, but are biblical imperatives the *blueprint of the divine will per se*? And should we think that immorality is found only in the Old Testament, we could point to the attitudes penned by our heroes of the New Testament, such as the degrading name-calling of scribes and Pharisees by Matthew, the anti-Semitic racism by John, or the sanctioned deaths of Ananias and Sapphira for deceiving the Spirit by Luke. A revised theology of the Bible

---

[A] Joshua 6; Judges 11:29–40; Exodus 34:6–7/Leviticus 26:39/Deuteronomy 5:8–10; 1 Samuel 15:2–3, 34; 2 Kings 2:23–25

is called for which is able to facilitate offensive biblical traditions without condoning them. To make the case that a *divine will* could have changed in time, or that biblical imperatives could have higher tariffs than moral conduct, will not do if it is believed that an immutable God has to behave better than any human being to have lived.[A]

A Book of Books

What do we find when we open the pages of the Bible? Ostensibly, it is a library of books covering Jewish and Christian history: it has pre-history, chronicles, poetry, oracles, prophecy, Gospels, letters and an Apocalypse. Structurally, the Bible covers the Creation, the origins of Judaism and the Christian revelation; it's an account of a monotheistic deity relating to *his people*. Many diverse books make up the Christian Bible; they represent various voices and different theologies to explain and address the human condition. The books of the Bible present no unified teaching, in spite of claims to the contrary. Various biblical theologies are discussed below in respect of the Creation myths, life after death, Jewish election, retributive justice and biblical prophecy.

A Bible of Different Voices

Origin of the Universe: Fact or Fable

Contentious debates between scientists and religionists over the origin of the universe and early mankind have occurred since the Enlightenment. Enlightened theologians and philosophers have no problem assimilating discoveries in modern science with biblical legends, because they see the place and purpose of cultural mythology, but there are still Creationists who try to preserve a false dichotomy of *scriptural authority* and *scientific evidence*. I don't wish to elaborate on this in detail now, but to look at the presuppositions upon which biblical views are often based.

Fallacious opinions are often voiced on whether the first eleven chapters of Genesis are records of history or products of mythology, whether the Hebrew sources predate the Babylonian Epics. The links are undoubtedly

---

[A] Matthew 24:50–51, 25:30, 46; Acts 5:1–11; Revelation 19:11–21

there, but they are fairly tenuous. An imperative question to ask is what point the authors were making through their utilisation of ancient myths.

The Creation Narratives

Scholars have traced three source traditions of Creation in the Bible:

1) the beginnings of the universe, animals and humankind (Genesis 1)[A]
2) the forming of the first man and woman (Genesis 2)[B]
3) the slaying of the primordial sea monster (Job, Isaiah, Psalms).[C]

Leviathan and Behemoth, William Blake   Epic of Gilgamesh Cuneiform Tablet

The Creation texts are separate units of literature, and only make sense if studied that way. The first Creation story focuses on the superior God of the Jews over rival deities (Yahweh over other tribal gods). The second is an etiological account of why humans have to die, the purpose and place of marriage, and the Fall and exclusion of humankind from paradise. The third involves a primeval struggle of Yahweh with a legendary monster,

---

[A] Genesis 1-2:3
[B] Genesis 2:4-25
[C] Job 26:12; Isaiah 51:9; Psalm 89:10 (*Rahab*)//Job 40:15, 19 (*Behemoth*) // Job 41:9, 25 (*Leviathan*)

an ancient myth that appears in Job, Isaiah and the Psalms. Yahweh had to slaughter *Leviathan*, *Rahab* and *Behemoth* to create the universe.[1]

> Was it not you who cut *Rahab* in pieces, who pierced the dragon?
> Was it not you who dried up the sea, the waters of the great deep?[A]

> Look at *Behemoth*, which I made just as I made you; it eats grass like an ox. Its strength is in its loins, and its power in the muscles… Can you draw out *Leviathan* with a fishhook, or press down its tongue?[B]

> God my King is from of old… You crushed the heads of *Leviathan*.[C]

The Flood

The biblical Flood narrative of Noah's Ark has also attracted attention in terms of parallel myths discovered in Canaanite, Ugaritic, Sumerian and Babylonian cultures.[2] It is the story of Yahweh destroying human beings to start afresh from the family of Noah. To endeavour to authenticate the 'worldwide' flood by evidence from geology and archaeology to *prove the Bible may be true* is to miss the point. Who wrote the biblical Flood story is not known, and most first-century Jews inheriting the traditional legend would have accepted it as a factual account (including Jesus and Paul).

Not only are there tenuous similarities in the various legends (the details of the ark covered in pitch, rescued family members, the collection of the animals, and the order of birds sent out to search for dry land), but there are also different theological purposes for the flood: for Noah, the flood was sent to destroy evil mankind; the Epic of Gilgamesh relates the quest of Utanapishtim for immortality after surviving a flood brought about at the whim of the Assembly of Gods (below). A cuneiform tablet with part of the Epic of Gilgamesh was discovered at Megiddo in Palestine, which suggests that the myth was widely known amongst the Jews.[3]

> Now the earth was *corrupt* in God's sight, and the earth was filled with

---

[A] Isaiah 51:9–10
[B] Job 38:4 – 41:1–2
[C] Psalm 74:12–17

violence. And God saw that the earth was corrupt; for *all flesh had corrupted its ways upon the earth.* And God said to Noah, 'I have determined to make an end of all flesh, for the earth is filled with violence because of them; now I am going to destroy them along with the earth.'[A]

Utanapishtim spoke to Gilgamesh, saying: 'I will reveal to you, Gilgamesh, a thing that is hidden, a secret of the gods I will tell you! Shuruppak, a city that you surely know, situated on the banks of the Euphrates, that city was very old, and there were gods inside it. *The hearts of the Great Gods moved them to inflict the Flood...*'

Forcing ancient narratives to comply with preconceived beliefs of what is expected in the *inspired* Scriptures will not be convincing for an enquiring mind of the modern world. To say that the authors of prehistory received transpersonal information of early beginnings before consciousness had evolved presupposes that the divine Creator once revealed something in a manner that never happens for most religious people today.

When we examine the literary conventions involved in the application of early biblical sources, it doesn't appear evident that any transpersonal factors were involved. Science and theology are not the same category of knowledge. To combine them in an ingenious method of synchronisation becomes a distraction from what they separately have to teach.

A revised theology of the biblical texts must not be reduced to redundant methodologies of conflating Scripture with modern science.

Life Beyond the Grave

The Bible doesn't have a consistent teaching of future life beyond death, but presents a series of contradictory opinions. It is recognised by critical scholars that Jewish views in the afterlife evolved during the Maccabean period, when Maccabean resistance fighters were executed and maimed in battle against the Seleucid forces.[4] The book of Daniel appeared at this time (165 BCE). Eternal life before this period was understood to be the eternal progeny of the Hebrew patriarchs. The New Testament upholds the teaching of physical resurrection at the return of Jesus (*Parousia*), Paul argued the case of physical resurrection, and the evangelists emphasised

---

[A] Genesis 6:11–12; Epic of Gilgamesh: Tablet 11:14

the physical nature of the resurrected Jesus through the empty tomb and appearance narratives. Examine these Hebrew passages of Scripture and observe the divergent theologies in the Christian Bible:

> What man can live and not see death? Can he deliver his soul from the power of *Sheol*? Selah [Psalm 89].[A]
>
> For *Sheol* cannot thank You, Death cannot praise You. Those who go down to the pit cannot hope for Your faithfulness [Isaiah 38].[B]
>
> For I know that my Redeemer lives, and that at the last he will stand upon the earth, and *after my skin has been thus destroyed*, then *in my flesh* I shall see God [Job 19]...[C]
>
> *Those who sleep in the dust* of the earth *shall awake*, some to *everlasting life*, and some to shame and *everlasting contempt* [Daniel 12].[D]
>
> But mortals die, and are laid low; humans expire, and where are they? As waters fail from a lake, and a river wastes away and dries up,
> > *so mortals lie down and do not rise again until the heavens are no more, they will not awake, or be roused out of their sleep* [Job 14].[E]
>
> Whoever is joined with all the living has hope, for a living dog is better than a dead lion. The living know that they will die, but *the dead* know nothing; *they have no more reward*, and even the memory of them is lost [Ecclesiastes 9].[F]

The resurrection of Jesus of Nazareth was central to the Christian Gospel. Inevitably, then, there are frequent references to life beyond the grave. I have discussed this fully elsewhere, but the point I make here is that the author of Ecclesiastes had no conception of a life beyond the grave.[5] And yet, the book of Ecclesiastes is in the Bible. We might conclude, therefore, that beliefs in a life hereafter developed over time in Judaism—from the progeny of the patriarchs, to an existence in the shadowy underworld of

---

[A] Psalm 89:48
[B] Isaiah 38:18
[C] Job 19:26
[D] Daniel 12:2
[E] Job 14:10–12
[F] Ecclesiastes 9:4–6

Sheol, to a physically raised body—which is plausible, supported through source tradition theory, and is theologically sound. However, the book of Ecclesiastes presents a radically different *voice* from that of the author of Daniel. The author of Job's speeches appears to hold contradictory views. The Bible is broadly thought by Christians to be *inspired* by God, and by inference have a *unified* teaching, yet a factor in a revised theology is that:

The Bible contains different, and contradictory, teachings of an afterlife.

No Foreigner Must Enter the Assembly of God

The descendants of Jacob (renamed Israel) are believed to be the 'chosen people'. Cultural threats to Jewish purity were condemned in the biblical books of Ezra and Nehemiah: they vocally disapproved of inter-marriage between Jews and foreigners, particularly for the tribe of Levi (Nehemiah assaulted Jewish offenders and pulled out their hair).[A] The Moabite and Ammonite tribes were castigated for not supporting the twelve tribes of Israel centuries ago when they moved to Canaan to inherit the 'promised land'. Moses condemned Israel for sexual relations with Moabite women and turning to the gods of Baal. A plague spread amidst the people until Phinehas, the grandson of Aaron, removed the curse by thrusting a spear into the Israelite offender and his Midianite harlot, an action reviewed in a Jewish Psalm as a deed of 'righteousness from generation to generation forever'.[B] And Nehemiah wrote:

> On that day they read from the book of Moses in the hearing of the people; and in it was found written that *no Ammonite or Moabite should ever enter the Assembly of God*, because they did not meet the Israelites with bread and water. When the people heard the law, *they separated from Israel all those of foreign descent*.[C]

The Story of Ruth: A Foreigner Accepted in Israel

The book of Ruth presents a radical challenge to the exclusive theology of the post-exilic reformers.

[A] Deuteronomy 23:3–4 // Nehemiah 13:23–25; Ezra 9:1–4, 10:1–12 (Numbers 23–24)
[B] Numbers 25; Psalm 106:30–31; Galatians 3:6
[C] Nehemiah 13:1–3

The book of Ruth begins when a Jew named Elimelech enters the land of Moab owing to a famine. He settles down, but dies, and his two sons take Moabite women to wed, thereby falling under the scorn of the reformers. After ten years, the two sons also die, and the matriarchal mother-in-law Naomi decides to return to her own country, and offers to take along her two daughters-in-law, but only Ruth travels to the land of Israel. As we follow the narrative we read about how Ruth gets married and enters the Jewish nation—she becomes a member of the *Assembly of God*. What is so compelling about the story is the author's emphasis on Ruth's ethnicity.

Ruth and Naomi, Jan Victors, 1653

We are told repeatedly that Ruth was a Moabite from the tribe of Moab. The point cannot be missed; it is a theological critique of Jewish elitism.[A] At the end of the book of Ruth the author drops a bombshell:

[A] Ruth 1:22, 2:2, 6, 21, 3:5, 10

Boaz took Ruth and she became his wife. When they came together, *the Lord made her conceive*, and she bore a son. The women of the neighbourhood gave him a name, saying, 'A son has been born to Naomi.' They named him Obed; he became the father of Jesse, the father of David.[A]

The husband of Ruth, 'the Moabite from the tribe of Moab', to stress, had been the father of Obed, the father of Jesse, the father of King David, the most celebrated monarch in Israelite history. A gauntlet has been tossed to Nehemiah and Ezra in reminding the Jewish purists that the ancestral tree of the house of David had passed through a woman of Moab.

The early Christians viewed themselves as the 'new Israel'—not that they adopted Judaism, but that they applied the special privilege and status of the 'chosen people' of God to the Christian Church through a redemptive action of Christ. Are we not compelled to ask whether such elitism as the chosen of God is appropriate in the modern age?

Should we discard any Christian self-designation as a special people as we seek a renewed theology of the Bible?

Retributive Justice

The book of Deuteronomy (literally, the 'second law') is the fifth book of the Pentateuch. In Hebrew tradition, Moses wrote this book, along with the preceding four books, Genesis, Exodus, Leviticus and Numbers (Jews regard them as the Torah, the Law). But, in the final form, Deuteronomy was completed during the reforms of King Josiah, the king of Judah.[6]

Chapter 28 presents a prescriptive list of the blessings and curses for the Israelite nation, blessings and curses resulting from the national conduct of Israel; the curses are explicitly outlined and outnumber the blessings by a ratio of three to one: the theology is called 'retributive justice'. Amos supports the principle of retributive justice:

Thus says the Lord: For three transgressions of Judah, and for four, *I will*

[A] Ruth 4:13–21

not revoke the punishment; because they have rejected the law of the Lord, and have not kept his statutes... So *I will send a fire on Judah, and it shall devour the strongholds of Jerusalem...*

Thus says the Lord: For three transgressions of Israel, and for four, *I will not revoke the punishment*; because they sell the righteous for silver, and the needy for a pair of sandals...[A]

Retributive justice was the overriding theology of Jewish and subsequent Christian Scripture. It was evident in the prophets (from Amos onwards) and the post-exilic reformers Ezra and Nehemiah. It exists in the books of the New Testament (Matthew, John, Revelation), and has featured within Christianity from the first century. The imperative of retributive justice is colloquially expressed as: honour God and all will be well, reject him and be wary of the consequence—we *reap what we sow*.

During the Exile, subsets of Jews were looking for an explanation of their captivity as a nation. The formulaic blessing contingency of putting away idols to serve Yahweh and assisting orphans and widows resonated with their current existential crisis. But there were other voices being sounded in Israel that are reflected in the books of Job, Proverbs and Ecclesiastes.

The Story of Job: Who is Responsible for Suffering?

The legend of Job turns the Deuteronomistic contingency programme of retributive justice on its head. We read of a wealthy Edomite (descendent of Esau) from the east who is robbed of his sons and daughters, servants, sheep, camels, oxen and donkeys at the whim of Satan to test his loyalty to Yahweh: to see whether he would eventually 'curse God and die'. This is not so much a legend of Hebrew folklore, since Job was not an Israelite, and neither were his three friends, who came from Arabia.[7]

The ancient legend takes us back to a time when the divine Council sat to consider the affairs of humanity. The prologue and epilogue (the earliest parts of Job) are where the theology of retributive justice is portrayed (as in the Koran). Job's fortunes return with more sons and daughters, twice

---

[A] Amos 2:4–16

the stock of animals and more wealth: is this not an objectionable form of justice—as if replacing the offspring of Job could compensate for what he had lost? Are we to reason that the first children of Job are unimportant? Throughout the narrative, Job is accepted as the most righteous person in the ancient world. He even offered sacrifices for his children in case they 'cursed God' during their partying.

Illustration to the Book of Job, William Blake, date unknown

In between the prologue and the epilogue are dialogues and monologues which comment on the meaning of human suffering. Three 'friends', the arbitrator and Yahweh discuss Job's plight (these debates represent some of the finest poetry in Jewish Wisdom literature). A discourse in Chapter 28 forms an interlude: the narrator raises a series of rhetorical questions, beginning with 'Where does Wisdom come from?', and culminating with the Almighty pronouncing His judgement from a whirlwind. The friends of Job give an explanation for Job's misfortune, and an arbitrator presents a summary before the Almighty, as the supreme Judge of the earth, gives the final verdict.

An early exchange occurs in the prologue between Satan and God about where the blame lay for the losses and sufferings of Job, but the epilogue clearly places it at the door of the Lord (Yahweh).

> Then there came to him all his brothers and sisters and all who had known him before, and they ate bread with him in his house; they showed him sympathy and comforted him for all *the evil that the Lord had brought upon him*...[A]

Job is recognised by every protagonist, and Yahweh, as a righteous soul.[B] Job challenges Yahweh to reveal his hand of justice. At times Job appears more just than the Almighty does, in spite of Elihu's protest. He requires an answer for why he has had to suffer and experience misfortune.[C] But merely *questioning the Lord* has rendered Job 'righteous [only] in his own eyes', as the arbitrator Elihu was forward to point out: Job believed that his own virtue had warranted prosperity and good fortune.[8]

The question the book of Job raises is whether the vicissitudes of life are just: whether God acts justly in the distribution of favour. After he voices his ignorance and loathes himself, Job's *eyes are opened to see Yahweh*. The story of Job serves as a critique of retributive justice. The author of John's Gospel illustrates that the theology of retributive justice continued well into the first century, that ailment and affliction were as a consequence of sins committed in the past, but the book of Job presents another *voice* in Israelite faith.[D] Job was not provided with an answer to unjust suffering, other than it being a feature of universal human experience, not resulting from the person's attitude and conduct.[9] Compare the Wisdom Sayings below from the books of Proverbs and Ecclesiastes:

[A] Job 2:9–10, 42:11
[B] Job 1:8, 22, 2:3, 10, 42:8
[C] Job 34:10–11, 29–31
[D] John 9:1–2

The Lord does not let the righteous go hungry, but he thwarts the craving of the wicked... *No harm happens to the righteous*, but the wicked are filled with trouble. Misfortune pursues sinners, but *prosperity rewards the righteous*.

In my vain life I have seen everything; *there are righteous people who perish in their righteousness*, and *there are wicked people who prolong their life* in their evildoing. Do not be too righteous, and do not act too wise; why should you destroy yourself?

There is a vanity that takes place on earth, that *there are righteous people who are treated according to the conduct of the wicked*, and *there are wicked people who are treated according to the conduct of the righteous*. I said that this also is vanity. So I commend enjoyment, for there is nothing better for people under the sun than to eat, and drink, and enjoy themselves, for this will go with them in their toil through *the days of life that God gives them* under the sun.[A]

In light of the predominant theology of retributive justice, how does the teaching of Jesus about a loving 'Heavenly Father' in the Sermon on the Mount speak to the reality of innocent suffering?

Prophetic Fulfilment

Authors of the Bible stress that God is true to his Word and honours his promises. Fundamentalist Christians rely on the promises of God in both Testaments. From the divine promises to Abraham of an eternal seed and land, to the promise to Samuel of the dynastic Messiah, to the promise to Ezekiel of the Jews returning to their homeland, to the promise of eternal life for the Christian believer at the *Parousia*.[B] The followers of Jesus had hoped for a kingdom on earth, and signs of its imminence were recorded in the apocalypses of the Synoptic Gospels and the book of Revelation, but is this early Christian belief credible from a historical perspective? Is it still plausible to interpret the Bible as a cryptic series of forecasts of the future that have been revealed to prophets and apostles of the Jewish and Christian traditions? Moses (allegedly) wrote the following:

[A] Proverbs 10:3; 12:21; 13:21/Ecclesiastes 7:15; 8:14
[B] Genesis 12:1–9; 2 Samuel 7:12–14; Ezekiel 37:12; 1 Thessalonians 4:13–18; Matthew 24:30–31; John 6:68

God is not a human being, that he should lie, or a mortal, that he should *change his mind*. Has he promised, and *will he not do it*? Has he spoken, and *will he not fulfil it*?[A]

The Story of Jonah: An Ambivalent God

The book of Jonah represents a different *voice* of prophetic forecasts. The story of Jonah was an improbable occurrence, but it illustrates a reversal of prophetic fulfilment. The narrative of Jonah is set during the Assyrian Empire. Sargon II (722–705 BCE) had devastated the northern kingdom of Israel, and his son Sennacherib (705–681 BCE) succeeded and ruled from the capital city of Nineveh. Although the prophecy of Jonah is set during the reign of Jeroboam II (783–741 BCE), the book was completed after the exile.[10] Jonah was a stubborn prophet who, similar to Abraham centuries before him, learned that the God of Israel sometimes *changes his mind*.[B]

Jonah was asked by God to pronounce judgement on the city of Nineveh, but he ran away from Yahweh and was caught up in a storm at sea. His crew yelled out in peril, but Jonah slept below deck. They prayed to their gods and cast lots to find out whom to blame. The souls of the mariners were at stake, and so Jonah (implausibly) offered his life as a ransom:

> Then the men were even more afraid, and said to him, 'What is this that you have done!' For the men knew that he was fleeing from the presence of the Lord, because he had told them so... He said to them, 'Pick me up and throw me into the sea; then the sea will quiet down for you; for I know *it is because of me* that this great storm has come upon you.'

The story of Jonah being swallowed by a sea monster and his frustration with God is well known, but what was the theological point of the story? Jonah offers to surrender his life on three occasions—he was entombed in the belly of the monster for three days and nights, and this made him an ideal prototype of Jesus for Matthew.[C]

[A] Numbers 23:19
[B] Jonah 4:2; Genesis 18:16–33; Jeremiah 18:7–10
[C] Matthew 12:39–40

The point of the narrative is to show that the God of Israel was capable of *repentance*, of changing his mind, a shock for those Israelites who viewed Yahweh as immutable and beyond waving. When the king and the lords of Nineveh *repented*, God averted judgement and spared the city, but this left Jonah angry. The Lord reproves Jonah, and tells him he has no right to begrudge his change of heart, even if the city of Nineveh has become an enemy of Israel:

> But this was very displeasing to Jonah, and he became angry. He prayed to the Lord and said, 'O Lord! Is not this what I said while I was still in my own country? That is why I fled to Tarshish at the beginning; for *I knew that you are a gracious God and merciful, slow to anger, and abounding in steadfast love*, and *ready to relent from punishing*. And now, O Lord, please take my life from me, for it is better for me to die than to live.' And the Lord said, 'Is it right for you to be angry?'

Jonah and the Whale, Pieter Lastman, 1621

The book of Jonah has a different message from other books of the Bible.

Roles are reversed; the sailors and the king of Nineveh appear to be more virtuous than Jonah is: the city of Nineveh was loathed by the Israelites, and was synonymous with evil, according to Nahum (612 BCE). The book of Jonah prescribes a different theology than those of the prophets Amos, Nahum, Malachi, and the reformers Nehemiah and Ezra. The prophecy of Jonah represents a *voice of toleration and acceptance* of the overlords of a dominant empire. It records a counter-message to the voices of the books of Daniel, the Jewish Apocalypses, and the Dead Sea Scrolls. The Bible doesn't have a monolithic message. It is a combined record of a series of disparate and diverse *voices*, one of which illustrates that Yahweh doesn't always act in the way anticipated or expected.

Is the path of history really predictable? Do certain people have access to the mind of God to divine future events? The author of Matthew thought so: he uses the entombment of Jonah as an analogy of the resurrection of Jesus, particularly the three-day-and-night burial in the monster's belly, but that is not to say that the tale of Jonah was written for that purpose.[A] What can we conclude about biblical prophecy from the book of Jonah? Are biblical forecasts fixed, or are they contingent upon the behaviour of the person/the people? And how should we interpret the forecasts in the Christian Bible which remain as yet unfulfilled?

A prophetic reference from Jeremiah claims that forecasts by Yahweh are contingent on human or national responsiveness:

> At one moment I may declare concerning a nation or a kingdom, that I will pluck up and break down and destroy it, but if that nation, concerning which I have spoken, turns from its evil, *I will change my mind* about the disaster that I intended to bring on it. And at another moment I may declare concerning a nation or a kingdom that I will build and plant it, but if it does evil in my sight, not listening to my voice, then *I will change my mind* about the good that I had intended to do to it.[B]

There are biblical passages that present an indecisive projection of God's

---

[A] Matthew 12:38–41
[B] Jeremiah 18:7–10

loyalty, then, and others that state emphatically that God always keeps to his word (as determined by the author).[11] Consider these biblical pledges:

> I will not leave you *until I have done what I have promised.* (Moses)
>
> *God is faithful*; by him you were called. (Paul)
>
> Thus *he has given us*, through these things, his precious and very *great promises*, so that through them you may escape from the corruption that is in the world because of lust, and may become participants of the divine nature. (Peter)[A]

One modern theologian has argued that God can do nothing without our response, that the Kingdom of God will not come unless Christians bring it about, which is an attempt to answer those who are hoping for a future apocalyptic event.[12] In light of the considerable delay in the *Parousia*, and against the beliefs of *inspired* authorities (e.g. Jesus of Nazareth, Paul, the evangelists, and the authors of Peter and Jude), we commend a renewed theology of the Bible.

The alternative hypothesis to prophetic determinism of fundamentalism is to interpret prophecy as the aspiration of each and every author or as a conditional contingency of human responsiveness.

In Summary

We cannot supply a definitive answer to the tensions and inconsistencies in the books of the Christian Bible. There will be Christians who consider it not necessary to form a renewed theology of the Bible on the basis that it has remained intact for over two millennia, and that writings *inspired* by God are not to be questioned. For such a view, I make two comments.

Firstly, the forming of a Christian canon was a tenuous process that had resulted after contentious arguments and counter-arguments over which documents to accept in the Bible, where power and politics had as much influence as scholarship. Secondly, disputes over books being *inspired* by God were arrived at by questionable criteria—whether it could be shown

---

[A] Genesis 28:15; 1 Corinthians 1:9; 2 Peter 1:4

as the work by an apostle—which failed to assess what was meant by the work having been *inspired* (or breathed) by God. How, for example could it be determined whether a document was or was not *divinely inspired*?

To formulate a renewed theology of the Christian Bible we have to begin with a few guiding principles that go part way to answering some of the reasonable objections that educated minds raise against Christian belief.[13] I commend the following to start such a process:

a) *A revised theology of the Christian Bible mustn't be reduced to methodologies of conflating Scripture with modern science.*

b) *It must acknowledge that the Bible has contradictory teachings of the afterlife.*

c) *It must reconcile the incongruent theologies of retributive justice and the conception of a 'Heavenly Father' in relation to innocent suffering.*

d) *A revised theology of the Bible should consider biblical prophecies not as the word of God per se, but as the aspiration of an author, or as a conditional contingency of human action.*

Notes

[1] For the lay reader, the sources can be seen in the titles of the deity: the term 'God' (*Elohim*) is used in the first Creation story, and in the second and third traditions the deity takes the name *Yahweh*. In the first Creation story God is omnipotent, in the second Yahweh is portrayed anthropomorphically, and in the references to a defeated sea monster, Yahweh is the victorious warrior.

[2] The mythological imagery derives from the Ugaritic sea monster *Lôtān* of the Baal cycle. The record of the Ugaritic myth has many gaps in the text, which render the meaning not very clear. The majority of scholars translate *Lôtān* as a 'fugitive serpent', the 'wriggling serpent', or 'the mighty one with seven heads', as depicted in the Syrian seals of the 18th–16th century BCE. Serpents feature prominently in the mythological iconography of the Ancient Near East: the

Sumerian depiction of *Ninurta* overcoming the seven-headed serpent (3rd millennium BCE). It was not uncommon in Near Eastern religion to include a sea monster in a cosmic battle between the forces of chaos and a creator god, or a cultural hero who imposes order by force. The Babylonian creation myth has *Marduk* defeating the serpent goddess *Tiamat*, whose body was divided to create the heavens and the earth. *Leviathan* is mentioned six times in the Bible (Job 3:8, 40:15–41:26, Amos 9:3, Psalm 74:13–23, Psalm 104:26 and Isaiah 27:1). Job 41:1–34 describes him in detail. Psalm 74 has God breaking the heads of *Leviathan* into pieces before giving his flesh to the people of the wilderness. Psalm 104 praises God for creating *Leviathan*, though Isaiah 27:1 calls him 'the tortuous serpent' who is to be killed at the end of the age. The term *Tannins* in the Genesis creation myth (translated as 'great whales' in the King James Version), and *Leviathan* in the Psalms are not presented as harmful but as ocean creatures of God's creation: the RSV footnote to Job 41:1 says that *Leviathan* may be a name for the crocodile; in a footnote to Job 40:15, it says that *Behemoth* may be a name for the hippopotamus. The element of competition between God and the sea monster and the inclusion of *Leviathan* to describe powerful enemies of Israel may reflect the influence of Mesopotamian and Canaanite legends.

3   Near Middle Eastern Flood epics come in three versions: the Sumerian *Epic of Ziusudra*, the Akkadian *Epic of Atrahasis*, and the Babylonian *Epic of Gilgamesh* featuring the hero Utnapishtim. The *Epic of Gilgamesh* has twelve tablets and is the most decipherable. The eleventh is a complete account of the flood: see below.

4   Ringgren 1974: 239–247, 322–324: see also 1 Maccabees 7:9, 14, 36, 12:43.

5   Lines 2017: 279–312.

6   Rogerson 2003: 153–154; Ringgren 1974: 5–8; Noth 1965: 273–280.

7   Only Job's daughters are given names, and they receive (counter-culturally) an inheritance at the close of the book (Job 42:13–15).

8   Job 32:1, 37:34: God is in control of the universe, and when he speaks from the whirlwind as the final discourse reaches the crescendo, he asks rhetorically who besides him can control *Behemoth* and *Leviathan*, the great sea monsters of antiquity: note how Yahweh does not permit Satan to destroy Job: 'Do not stretch out your hand against him' (Job 1:12, 2:6). Satan's only power was to afflict Job's skin with sores.

9   One thing is clear from the narrative of Job. In stark contrast to the theologies of Amos and the prophets, Deuteronomy, Ezra and Nehemiah, fortune and prosperity is not contingent on virtue, the answer of divine retributive justice doesn't comply with human experience: God acts mysteriously in a complex world. Is it true that God rewards virtue and brings evil upon vice? The Bible doesn't provide a consistent theology on such outcomes as virtuous or evil conduct, but has contradictory teachings.

10 Philological study illustrates that the book of Jonah has words and phrases of late Hebrew and Aramaic influence: these factors, and the historical situation the book presupposes, imply the work was completed around the late fifth or early fourth century BCE: *Mercer's Dictionary of the Bible*: 465, *Encyclopaedia Britannica*, and *Asbury Commentary*, 'Part II: Historical Setting, Authorship, and Date of Jonah'.

11 The whole narratives of the Pentateuch are based upon this theology, we find it in many of the prophetic sayings, and it is the basis of Christian hope. It is evident, as I have argued elsewhere, that the historical Jesus, like the Baptist before him, believed the end of the age and the arrival of the Kingdom would occur in his own lifetime. Paul believed that he would be caught up in the rapture at the return of Jesus (1 Thessalonians 4:17). The letters of Jude and Peter kept alive that hope (albeit by stretching out the time period), and it is the foundation of the book of Revelation (Matthew 11:3/Luke 7:18–19; Mark 9:1, 13:30; Matthew 10:23; 2 Thessalonians 4:17; 2 Peter 3:1–9; Jude 14–15).

12 I refer to J. Crossan's 'collaborative eschatology': an eschatological dialectic between the human and divine. Many books by Crossan cover his theology. He argues that the Kingdom of God will not arrive as a future eschatological event, but by Christians taking on vocations of healing (spiritual healing), as Jesus did by sending his apostles through the villages of Lower Galilee. Jesus accepted John the Baptist's teaching that viewed the Kingdom as imminent, but changed his mind after he was killed. Jesus viewed God as ever present, but because John had not been rescued by God, he deduced that the Kingdom must be already here and now. Thus, 'it is not that we are waiting for God, it is that God is waiting for us': Beilby and Eddy 2010: 125.

13 The New Testament texts that are often quoted are 2 Timothy 3:16–17 (a book of doubted Pauline authorship), 2 Peter 1:20–21 (a book widely considered to be late and not authored by Peter) and the book of Revelation 1:3, 22:18–19. It is

totally unconvincing for a biblical author to claim that his work, and, by extension, every other book that (more by serendipity than design) happened to find its way into the Christian canon, is 'inspired by God'. Paul certainly didn't think his letters were 'inspired by God'. Other references often quoted are Joshua 1:8, 23:6, Isaiah 40:8, Luke 16:17, and 2 Peter 3:15

Links of the Epic of Gilgamesh with the Biblical Flood

Gilgamesh spoke to Utanapishtim, the Faraway: "I have been looking at you, but your appearance is not strange—you are like me!
You yourself are not different—you are like me!
My mind was resolved to fight with you,
(but instead?) my arm lies useless over you.
Tell me, how is it that you stand in the Assembly of the Gods, and have found life!"

Utanapishtim spoke to Gilgamesh, saying: "I will reveal to you, Gilgamesh, a thing that is hidden, a secret of the gods I will tell you!
Shuruppak, a city that you surely know, situated on the banks of the Euphrates, that city was very old, and there were gods inside it.
The hearts of the Great Gods moved them to inflict the Flood.
(Genesis 6:6–13)

Their Father Anu uttered the oath (of secrecy),
Valiant Enlil was their Adviser,
Ninurta was their Chamberlain,
Ennugi was their Minister of Canals.
Ea, the Clever Prince(?), was under oath with them so he repeated their talk to the reed house: 'Reed house, reed house! Wall, wall!
O man of Shuruppak, son of Ubartutu:
Tear down the house and build a boat! (Genesis 6:14)
Abandon wealth and seek living beings!

Spurn possessions and keep alive living beings!
Make all living beings go up into the boat. (Genesis 6:16)
The boat which you are to build,
its dimensions must measure equal to each other:

its length must correspond to its width.
Roof it over like the Apsu… (Genesis 6:15–16)

I provided it with six decks… (Genesis 6:16)
Three times 3,600 (units) of raw bitumen I poured into the
bitumen kiln, three times 3,600 (units of) pitch …into it… (Genesis 6:14)
The boat was finished by sunset…

All the living beings that I had I loaded on it, (Genesis 6:19)
I had all my kith and kin go up into the boat, (Genesis 6:18)
all the beasts and animals of the field and the craftsmen I had go up…
(Genesis 6:19–20)

Just as dawn began to glow
there arose from the horizon a black cloud… Erragal pulled out the mooring
poles, forth went Ninurta and made the dikes overflow. (Genesis 7:11)

No one could see his fellow, they could not recognize each other in the
torrent. The gods were frightened by the Flood, and retreated, ascending to
the heaven of Anu. The gods were cowering like dogs, crouching by the
outer wall… How could I say evil things in the Assembly of the Gods,
ordering a catastrophe to destroy my people!!

Six days and seven nights came the wind and flood, the storm flattening the
land. (Genesis 7:4, 20)
When the seventh day arrived, the storm was pounding, the flood was a
war-struggling with itself like a woman writhing (in labour).
The sea calmed, fell still, the whirlwind (and) flood stopped up.
I looked around for coastlines in the expanse of the sea,
and at twelve leagues there emerged a region (of land).
On Mount Nimush the boat lodged firm,
Mount Nimush held the boat, allowing no sway… (Genesis 7:4)

When a seventh day arrived (Genesis 7:10)
I sent forth a dove and released it.
The dove went off, but came back to me; no perch was visible,
so it circled back to me. (Genesis 7:8–9)

I sent forth a swallow and released it.
The swallow went off, but came back to me; no perch was visible so it circled back to me. I sent forth a raven and released it.
The raven went off, and saw the waters slither back. (Genesis 7:7–8)
Then I sent out everything in all directions and sacrificed (a sheep). (Genesis 7:17–20) I offered incense in front of the mountain-ziggurat. (Genesis 7:21)
Seven and seven cult vessels I put in place, and (into the fire) underneath (or: into their bowls) I poured reeds, cedar, and myrtle.
The gods smelled the savour, the gods smelled the sweet savour, and collected like flies over a (sheep) sacrifice." (Genesis 7:21)

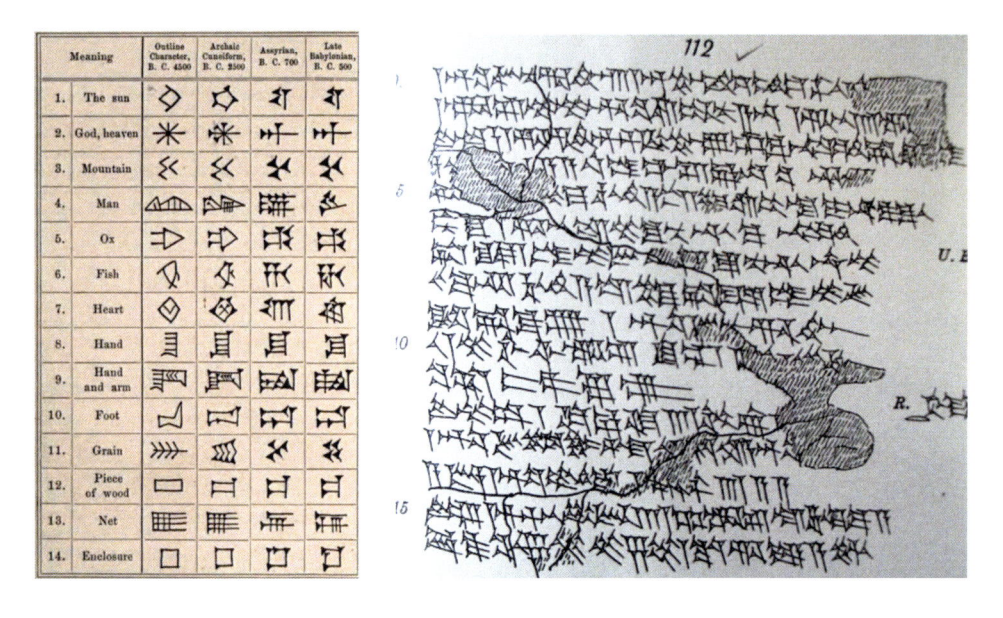

Cuneiform Alphabetic Script: Words and Sayings

http://www.ancienttexts.org/library/mesopotamian/gilgamesh/tab11.htm

Afterthought

The dedication commended the importance of Christian spirituality and rational empiricism. It may seem a contradiction in terms initially, but it's a paradox. Many issues surrounding religion are paradoxical. Indeed the biblical narratives contain examples of paradox. Since the Enlightenment, the rational processes of deduction and empirical evidence have formed the conceptual framework of western mentality, and this works well on a superficial level of research until we come to *paradoxical events* in history. The Christian Scriptures preserve traditions of paradoxical conundrums. These were once described as *signs* and *wonders* (miracles) in ancient days to conform to primitive worldviews.

In the narrative of Abraham in Hebrew tradition, he put his confidence in an unknown God and went into a strange country, but eastern nomads of the time wouldn't venture to foreign lands unless they were known to be fertile and free of conflict. Moses turned towards a burning shrub that was not consumed to address the paradoxical God without name calling him to free up the Hebrew slaves from Egypt, but burning shrubs soon become ash, and powerful rulers of empires never release their sources of labour. God would later be known as *Yahweh*: *He who brings into existence, what exists*. These were paradoxical *events*. If Abraham and Moses hadn't existed, their histories have been firmly grounded in Jewish tradition.

Jesus of Nazareth healed the sick by word of mouth, but diseased people cannot be cured without biochemical treatments. Jesus had been crucified as a criminal of Rome, and became the Saviour of the world, but executed criminals can hardly be Saviours of anything. Christianity was founded upon a belief that Jesus came from the dead, but dead people don't come back to life. These were paradoxical *events*. An *indisputable fact* in history is that Christianity not only spread and became the major religion of the Roman Empire, it was formed on the basis of *impossible happenings*.

How are we to reconcile the paradox of faith and empirical rationality? We could simply elect to sit comfortably within a camp of 'blind faith', or conversely remain assured by the evidence deduced through empiricism.

In each case, we are avoiding the paradox, rather than addressing it and seeing it as an existential truth. So, what do I mean by existential truth?

The word *existential* means 'to substantiate the existence of a thing'. If we can appreciate the paradoxical nature of human existence and affirm that *meaning* can be found in the historical *continuum* of time and place, then we are living in what Paul understood as 'faith' (*trust*), not by artificially accepting bodies of dogmatic beliefs, but by validating *spiritual experience*. This is neither intuitive, nor is it established through systematic testing. Empirical *truths* can be receptive to objective testing and experimentation through scientific methodologies, but history is rarely accessible for such methods. History at the superficial level can be verified, in that empirical *facts* can be confirmed by evidence from documented source material and archaeology, but, at the higher level of seeking *meaning* within those *facts*, the exercise becomes subjective: it is informed by a particular theory that is utilised to make sense of the empirical *facts* of the where and when of history. The empirical methodologies are also redundant in other areas.

In the areas of morality, spirituality, art, aesthetics and poetry, empirical rationality is of little use. Such disciplines are inaccessible for the rational method of logical deduction. Social *morality* is an example where there is no universal agreement over the death penalty, or the age of consent for sexual relations. A nation might make a criminal offence of an anti-social action that had once been permitted: slavery in Britain had been justified on religious grounds, but now is judged as a criminal offence. *Spirituality* is also a relative term that describes a wide range of activities. How can a researcher analyse, through methods of empirical testing, an *experience* of *spiritual conversion*, *spiritual renewal*, or *spiritual bliss*, in psychological and behavioural terms?

Christians see *meaning* behind particular *events* in Jewish history: that the Galilean prophet executed at the hand of a Roman official in the early 30s was *experienced* by his closest followers to be ever-present with them in a way which is impossible to evaluate, or to authenticate in rational terms. The effects of that *experience*—the beginning of a dynamic religion which was to take over the Roman Empire—cannot be refuted, and neither can the effect of that current *experience* be invalidated for a devotee. Particular *events* which occur in time and place can be claimed to be neutral within our historical paradigm, but we could equally claim that that *event* has a *meaning* far and above the empirical evidence that it had once happened in a particular time and place: the person's *experience* becomes authentic, albeit subjective and interpretive. For the committed Christian, Jesus has not only risen from the dead, but still lives on. A final question, therefore, is in what sense a belief of Jesus *being alive again* is understood, if not in a physical way, in what way?

The Christian Bible has served as 'evidence' of historical *events* of ancient periods occurring. It was believed that if accounts of the *events* were read in the Bible, they must have happened in the way they are portrayed. But two centuries of biblical criticism have illustrated that the Bible cannot be self-validating of historical *events*: the argument is circular. What, then, is the relevance of forms of Christianity dependant on the Bible today? This book has purposely circumvented the relevance of the modern churches, denominations and sects etc., because such communities are institutional organisations which have their origins in history, which have developed to meet particular historical and social needs. Our study of the authentic Pauline letters has illustrated how the early Jesus communities (*ecclesias*) were more fluid than most conventional churches of today, but, then, the first-generation Jesus believers were living within the context of the end of the age. Not many religious communities commit to this view today, I suspect, at least in practice if in belief.

The Bible is conventionally used as the *holy text* in worship and reflection in Christian liturgy, but it has hardly any prominence in secular debates on moral and social issues today. Church attendance is declining, and the average ages of members are becoming older. Secularism, hedonism and monetarism are having greater influence in western society, particularly for the young. Evangelical fundamentalists barely recognise the paradox of religious belief and empiricism (it is subsumed in doctrinaire naïveté), whilst the paradox for staunch traditionalists of high churches is known, but resisted (which results in bigoted forms of conservatism). Although our western culture remains indebted to the heritage of the (KJV) Bible, it has become an anachronistic relic of the past for the majority. My reason for writing this book has been to contribute towards arresting the decline and revive a dwindling interest in biblical study with broader theological objectivity. Paul once addressed the crisis of his time by re-evaluating the teaching of Jesus beyond the parameters of Jewish Law for a non-Jewish world. He served as the ideal forerunner of the Radical Gospel.

Subject and Author Index

Abraham 57.
Acts of Thecla 44–45.
Alexander the Great 14–15.
Apocalypse 61, 103–105.
Apocalypse of Peter 125–127.
Apocryphal Gospels 125–128.
Apollo 14.
Apostolic Constitutions 126.
Areopagus 51–52.
Arrest of Jesus 121–122.
Athens 51–51, 62.

Behemoth 148.
Beker (J.C.) 139.
Birth Narratives 117–118.
Bornkamm (G.) 8, 10, 54, 72, 139.
Brown (R.E.) 100–101.
Bruce (F.F.) 138.
Bujard (W.) 139.

Caesar Augustus (Octavian) 5, 9,
   11–20, 35–36, 40–49, 58, 94, 98.
Caird (J.B.) 109.
Canon (of Scripture) 162.
Celsus 26–27.
Christian expansion 24–26, 31–32,
   33.
Christian Mission 4, 52–53.
Christians (Hellenistic) 6, 9, 72.
Christians (Jewish) 6, 9.
Christology 98–101, 107–108.
Chrysostom 25.
Circumcision 77.
Civil War (Rome) 11, 36.
Cleopatra 11–13, 98.

Constantine (Emperor) 21–34, 62.
Crossan (J.D.) 8, 20, 38-39, 161.
Crucifixion Narratives 119–121.

David (King of Israel) 56
Diocletian (Emperor) 27.
Divinity of Jesus 95–101.

Ecclesia/s 26–27, 31, 38.
Ehrman (B.D.) 8, 30, 60, 61, 90, 101,
   136.
Emperor worship 5, 18.
Emperors 19, 32, 36.
Ephesus 35–36, 42, 139.
Epic of Gilgamesh 149, 163–164.
Eusebius 24.

Forgery (of Manuscripts) 125–141.

Galen 125.
Gamaliel 70.
God–fearers (Gentiles) 4, 58, 59,
   65–84.
Gospel Sources 111–115, 125–128.
Gospel (Pauline) 7, 36–50, 58, 111.
Gospel Authenticity 111–122.
Gospel of Peter 126–128, 141–142.
Goulder (M.D.) 8.
Greco–Roman Religion 4, 18, 23.

Harnack (A. von) 24, 25.
Heavenly Powers/Angels 101–105,
   137–141.
Heiser (S.M.) 101.
Historical Jesus 6, 59–60.

James (brother of Jesus) 8.
Jerusalem church 8, 67, (65–84).
Jewish diaspora 4, 38–39.
Jewish Messiah 9, 28, 54–58.
Julius Caesar 11, 13, 94, 98.

Kosher 5, 6, 65–84.

Legends/Myths (Biblical and non–biblical) 146–150, 155.
Leviathan 148–150.
Luther (M.) 132.

Mark Antony 11–13.
Mill (J.) 114–115.
Miracles (Christian) 101–106, 109, 118.

Nero 19, 129.
Nicene Creed 95–101, 106.
Noah's Flood 149–150.

Paganism (Greco–Roman polytheism) 89–93.
Parousia (Advent of Jesus) 9, 61, 131, 137, 151, 158, 161.
Paul/Saul of Tarsus 4, 35, 47–49, 51–63, 65–84.

Pauline (Authentic Letters) 3–6, 35–48, 130–139.
Persecution (Christian) 28–30.
Peter (Simon, *Cephas*) 8, 27, 67–68, 77, 81–82.
Pharisees 3, 4, 53, 62, 70, 73.
Philo of Alexandria 4, 107.
Philosophies 51–52, 63.
Plato 141.
Radical Gospel: ethnicity 37–41.

Radical Gospel: gender 44–47.
Radical Gospel: slavery 41–44.
Reed (J.L.) 8.
Rehab 148.
Roman Administration 11–20.
Roman Amphitheatres 17, 67.
Roman Church 38.
Roman coinage 16.
Roman Empire 4, 11–20, 35, 58.

Sabbath 5.
Saul of Tarsus (background) 3–5.
Scripture/s (Christian) 131–140.
Slavery 41–44, 48.
Son of God 9, 19–20, 34–35, 94, 96.

Tarsus 4.
Theodosius (Emperors I and II) 29–30, 34.
Torah (Mosaic Law) 3, 6, 57–58, 62, 65–84.

Wright (N.T.) 8, 143–144.

Yahweh (*Kyrios*) 9, 36, 56, 146, 148, 155–157.

Biblical Page Index

Hebrew Scriptures | Book Page References

Genesis	57, 147.
Deuteronomy	57, 154.
Ruth	152–154.
Ezra	152.
Nehemiah	152.
Job	151, 155–157.
Ecclesiastes	151, 157.
Isaiah	4, 58–59.
Jeremiah	161.
Daniel	151, 154.
Amos	154–155.
Jonah	158–161.

Christian Scriptures | Book Page References

Matthew	4, 59, 101, 118.
Mark	97–98, 100, 106, 113–114, 118, 121–122.
Luke	6, 52–53, 54, 58, 59, 65–84, 101.
John	98, 121–122.
Acts	4, 6, 24, 27, 54, 55, 65–84.
Romans	26, 46, 54, 60, 96, 105, 139.
1 & 2 Corinthians	26, 27, 28, 34, 49–50, 62.
Galatians	38, 57, 60, 65–84.
Ephesians	43–44, 46, 105, 137–140.
Philippians	62.
Colossians	43–44, 46, 105, 140.
1 & 2 Thessalonians	22, 61, 62, 96, 135–137.
1 & 2 Timothy	44, 46–47, 132–135.
Titus	44, 46–47, 133–135.
Philemon	42–43, 48.
1 & 2 Peter	128–131.

Other publications by the author include:

You Say That I Am: The Historical Jesus Becomes the Messiah
Spirituality in Counselling and Psychotherapy
The Bullies: The Rationale of Bullying
Brief Counselling in Schools

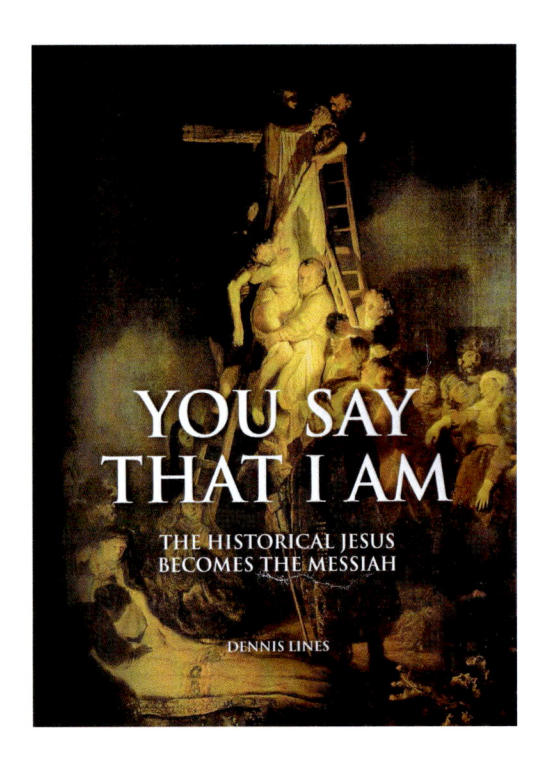

The author contends that the Gospels are not a mirror, but provide a reliable snapshot of the historical Jesus in Galilee. He delivered a radical message of the Kingdom of God, which involved an apocalyptic drama at the end of the age, and that this would occur in his own day.

Dennis Lines asks whether the calling of Jesus can still be tenable for people today. Is it feasible to hold a view that Jesus was the Jewish Messiah to save humankind if he never claimed to be the chosen Messiah, the Son of Man, or the Son of God, in his lifetime? Could he become these titles as an *existential vision in retrospective reflection*?

References

Aslan D. (2014) *Zealot: The Life and Times of Jesus of Nazareth*. New York: Random House.

Beilby J.K. and Eddy P.R. (Editors) (2010) *The Historical Jesus: Five Views*. London: SPCK Publishing.

Beker J.C. (1980) *Paul The Apostle: The Triumph of God in Life and Thoughts*. Philadelphia: Fortress.

Borg M.J and Crossan J.D. (2009) *The First Paul: Reclaiming the Radical Visionary Behind the Church's Conservative Icon*. London: SPCK.

Bornkamm G. (1971) *Paul*. New York: Harper and Row.

Brown R.E. (1957) 'Does the New Testament call Jesus God?'. *The Scottish Journal of Theological Studies* 10: 545–572.

Brown R.E. (1994) *An Introduction to New Testament Christology*. Paulist Press: New York.

Bruce F.F. (1999) *Paul: Apostle of the Heart Set Free*. Grand Rapids, MI: Eerdmans.

Bujard W. (1973) *Stilanalytische Untersuchungen zum Kolosserbrief: Als Beitrag zur Methodik von Sprachvergleichen*. Gottingen: Vandenhoeck & Ruprecht.

Bultmann R. (1955) The Christological Confession of the World Council of Churches, *Essays Philosophical and Theological*. New York: 273-90.

Carrier R. (2012) *Proving History: Bayes's Theorem and the Quest for the Historical Jesus*. Sheffield: Prometheus Books.

Carrier R. (2014) *On the Historicity of Jesus: Why We Might Have Reason for Doubt*. Sheffield: Sheffield Phoenix Press.

Conzelmann H. (1976) *An Outline of the Theology of the New Testament*. London: SCM Press.

Crossan J.D. (1993) *The Historical Jesus: The Life of a Mediterranean Jewish Prophet*. New York: HarperOne.

Crossan J.D. (1998) *The Birth of Christianity: Discovering What Happened in the Years Immediately After the Execution of Jesus*. New York: HarperOne.

Crossan J.D. (2008) *God and Empire: Jesus Against Rome, Then and Now*. New York: HarperOne.

Crossan J.D. and Reed J.L. (2005) *In Search of Paul: How Jesus' Apostle Opposed Rome's Empire with God's Kingdom*. London: SPCK.

Dawkins R. (2006, 2016) *The God Delusion*. London: Black Swan (Penguin Random House).

Dibelius M. (1956) *Studies in the Acts of the Apostles*. London: SCM.

Ehrman B.D. (2003) *Lost Christianities: The Battles for Scripture and the Faiths We Never Knew*. New York: Oxford University Press.

Ehrman B.D. (2005) *Misquoting Jesus: The Story Behind Who Changed the Bible and Why*. New York: Harper Collins.

Ehrman B.D. (2012) *FORGED: Writing in the Name of God: Why the Bible's Authors Are Not Who We Think They Are*. New York: HarperOne.

Ehrman B.D. (2012) *The New Testament: A Historical Introduction to the Early Christian Writings* (5th Ed.). New York: Oxford University Press.

Ehrman B.D. (2018) *The Triumph of Christianity: How a Forbidden Religion Swept the World*. New York: Simon and Schuster.

Elliott J.K. (1993) *Apocryphal New Testament*. Lewisville: Westminster and John Knox, 1991–92.2: 493–94.

Everitt A. (2007) *Augustus: The Life of Rome's First Emperor*. London: Random House Trade.

Farmer W.R. (1976) *The Synoptic Problem: A Critical Analysis*. Macon GA: Mercer.

Goulder M. (2009) *A Tale of Two Missions*. London: SCM.

Harnack A. von (1908) *The Expansion of Christianity in the First Three Centuries* (Vol. 2, trans. James Moffatt). New York: G.P. Putnam's Sons.

Harris W. (1989) *Ancient Literacy*. Cambridge, MA: Harvard University Press.

Harrison A.N. (1921) *The Problem of the Pastoral Epistles*. Oxford: Oxford University Press.

Heiser S.M. (2015) *The Unseen Realm: Recovering the Supernatural Worldview of the Bible*. Bellingham, WA: Lexham Press.

Heiser S.M. (2017) *Reversing Hermon: Enoch, the Watchers and the Forgotten Mission of Jesus Christ*. Crane, MO: Defender Publishing.

References

Hitchens C. (2008) *God is Not Great: How Religion Poisons Everything*. London: Atlantic Books.

Hölscher T. (2006) 'The Transformation of Victory into Power: From Event to Structure'. In S. Dillon and K.E. Welch (2006) *Representations of War in Ancient Rome*. Cambridge: CUP. 27-48.

Hurtado L.A. (2006) *The Earliest Christian Artefacts: Manuscripts and Christian Origins*. Cambridge, UK: William B. Eerdmans Publishing Company.

Koester H. (2000) *History and Literature of Early Christianity, Introduction to the New Testament* (Vol. 2). Berlin: Walter de Gruyter & Co.

Kümmel W.G. (1974) *The Theology of the New Testament: According to its Major Witnesses Jesus-Paul-John*. London: SCM Press Ltd.

Lines D. (2017) *You Say That I Am*. Rubery, Birmingham: Lines.

McHaffie A. and McHaffie I. (2010) *All One in Christ Jesus*. Edinburgh: Ian and Averil McHaffie.

Noth M. (1965) *The History of Israel*. London: Adam & Charles Black.

Price R.M. (2000) *Deconstructing Jesus*. New York: Prometheus Books.

Ringgren H. (1974) *Israelite Religion*. London: SPCK.

Rogerson J.W. (2003) 'Deuteronomy'. In J.D.G. Dunn and J.W. Rogerson (2003) *Eerdmans Commentary on the Bible*. Grand Rapids, MI: Eerdmans.

Schleiermacher F. (1807). Referenced in Elliott J.K (1993).

Stein R.H. (2001) *The Synoptic Problem: An Introduction*. Grand Rapids, MI: Baker Academic.

Williams C.S.C. (1975) *A Commentary on the Acts of the Apostles*. London: Adam & Charles Black.

Williams C. (1975): Referenced in Dibelius (1956).

Wright N.T. (2018) *Paul: A Biography*. London SPCK.